Contemporary
Spanish Culture

Contemporary Spanish Culture

TV, Fashion, Art and Film

Paul Julian Smith

polity

First published in 2003 by Polity Press in association with Blackwell Publishers Ltd, a Blackwell Publishing Company.

Editorial office:
Polity Press
65 Bridge Street
Cambridge CB2 1UR, UK

Marketing and production:
Blackwell Publishers Ltd
108 Cowley Road
Oxford OX4 1JF, UK

Published in the USA by
Blackwell Publishers Inc.
350 Main Street
Malden, MA 02148, USA

ISBN 0-7456-3052-9
ISBN 0-7456-3053-7   (pbk)

A catalogue record for this book is available from the British Library and has been applied for from the Library of Congress.

Typeset in 10.5 on 12 pt Plantin
by Graphicraft Limited, Hong Kong
Printed in Great Britain by MPG Books, Bodmin, Cornwall

This book is printed on acid-free paper.

Contents

List of Illustrations

Acknowledgements

I would like to thank John Thompson at Polity for his efficiency and warm encouragement of this project. For providing illustrations and permissions I thank Telecinco, Adolfo Domínguez SA, Fundació la Caixa and DACS (for Barceló), Txomin Badiola, Films la Rambla (for Ventura Pons) and El Deseo (for Almodóvar). Every attempt has been made to trace copyright holders. The author and publishers would like to apologize in advance for any inadvertent use of copyright material.

I am most grateful to friends and colleagues in Spain whose invitations gave me the opportunity to undertake research in Barcelona, Bilbao and Madrid. This book is dedicated to the staff, both academic and assistant, and students (especially graduate students) in Cambridge during my decade as Professor and Head of Department, 1991–2001.

Paul Julian Smith
London and Cambridge, 2002

Introduction: Cultures of Distinction

The issue of *Newsweek* magazine dated 17 September 2001 featured on its cover Spanish fashion house Zara. While the terrible events of that week were to make fashion seem even more trivial and futile than it is generally held to be, the cover remains significant. Many of us who work on Spanish culture complain that it is marginalized by the media. But in this case one aspect of Spanish visual culture was unusually prominent. The British national press had already called attention to the Zara label with the claim that 'Spanish chic [was] cutting a dash across the world' (Rosier 2001). There were intriguing aspects to the story. Zara is based in what the journalist calls the 'unlikely surroundings of north western Spain'. Yet it is highly advanced, both aesthetically and economically, 'delivering cosmopolitan, catwalk-style chic' through production processes that take only a few weeks from design to sale (most UK manufacturers take the best part of a year). Moreover, unlike makes of other brands who scour the world for the cheapest labour, Zara has built its global success on fidelity to a local work force. Owning outright both the stores and the workshops situated mainly in its native Galicia, Zara is, in the industry jargon, 'vertically integrated' with a vengeance. Production is adapted on a daily basis according to sales: the supply chain is demand- rather than supply-led. While much recent cultural theory has claimed that consumption now takes precedence over production, for Zara the customer really is king.

The case of Zara (like that of fellow fashion house Adolfo Domínguez, to which I devote a chapter) thus points to some important questions relating to the three terms I use in the title of this book. First, where do we place the limits of 'contemporary' culture, now that the old divisions between high and low have been erased? Television and fashion, for example, are so closely integrated into modern life that they seem all-pervasive, almost impossible to analyse. Secondly, what is 'Spanish' culture? Many of the most dynamic examples of what is often held to be Spanish are produced by the historic nationalities of the Basque Country, Catalonia and Galicia. Yet it is precisely those distinct cultures (often invisible to outsiders: the journalist fails to mention Galicia in his article) that, far from being parochial, may have the most global reach. Finally, how do we decide which objects of this newly expanded and localized 'culture' are worthy of study? In this book I focus on cultural products which (like Zara's 'cosmopolitan catwalk-style') benefit from 'distinction', the cultural value acquired through a social process that is normally hidden from view. While my definition of distinction derives from French sociologist Pierre Bourdieu, a research team headed by Spanish urbanist Manuel Castells suggested over ten years ago that 'mov[ing] aggressively into higher quality markets' (Benton 1989: 229) was the right strategy for medium-sized nations such as Spain.

This book, then, initiates a venture, or adventure, into new objects of study, new fields. Media such as television and fashion have received relatively little attention, particularly in relation to 'content', i.e. actual programmes and garments. Visual arts, relatively better known, have been read either in abstract, theoretical terms or in financial, institutional terms, the first approach being complicit with the artist, the second with the art market. I hope to mediate between the two approaches. Cinema, on the other hand, has received extensive study from academic critics in Spain, the UK and the USA. My aim here, however, is to combine the economic and the aesthetic in the study of two kinds of distinction: 'independent films' and 'art movies'.

In recent years a number of books have been published in the wake of Graham's and Labanyi's ground-breaking *Spanish Cultural Studies: An Introduction* (1995).[1] These collective volumes testify to a widespread feeling that Hispanic studies can no longer continue as a literary specialization, but must embrace wider and more dynamic media. While each of these books is welcome, in that together they have helped to establish a radically new field, they pay little or no sustained attention to some of the media studied here. More importantly, perhaps, they have no consistent approach to contemporary Spanish culture, as each contributor writes from his or her own theoretical perspective. In a new discipline, newly urgent questions arise. How are those of us trained in literary or film studies to address other visual media? And which approach is most useful? We need both to pay attention to the specificity of each medium (what makes TV or fashion unique) and to attempt a general analysis of culture (what visual arts and cinema may be said to share).

Since much of my primary material will be unfamiliar to readers, I adopt a single explanatory format for each chapter, moving consistently from the general to the particular. Beginning with a broad account of problems in each field ('How do we approach TV?'; 'What does it mean to call a film "independent"?'), I go on to give accounts of the field in Spain, of a single producer within that national field and, finally, of particular works. The broad account of problems at the start of each chapter often derives from the Anglo-American sources who have generally originated and developed debates on such terms as 'quality' television and 'conceptual' art. These paradigms are then tested against Spanish practices, which frequently challenge or contradict them. For example, Almodóvar's 'art movies' are massively popular at the box office in their home country, unlike their North American equivalents. Moreover, what does it mean to say 'art movie' in Spain, when in the USA the term is often synonymous with 'foreign language film'?

What I hope to show is that in all the media I treat, Spain has in the last decade made a distinctive contribution that has not yet been fully recognized. Spanish television (chapter 1), generally scorned by Spaniards themselves, is in fact one of the biggest producers of series drama in Europe, overtaking France and Germany and selling original formats abroad. Likewise Spanish fashion (chapter 2), based as we have seen in the rural region of Galicia and lacking the high profile of the Italian clothing industry, is now exported globally. Mallorcan painter Miquel Barceló (chapter 3), wunderkind of the 1980s, is an established star of the international art market, while Basque artists (chapter 4), often trained in New York or London, investigate the fashionable themes of sex and gender with a distinct edge. Ventura Pons (chapter 5), Catalonia's favoured filmmaker, shows his highly crafted feature films at the most prestigious festivals world-wide, while Pedro Almodóvar (chapter 6), Spain's consecrated *auteur*, has combined commercial and critical success (notably a recent Oscar and BAFTA) by moving up-market into a higher cultural register. Based on new empirical research, this book pays close attention to commercial practices of production, offering six case studies of these major players in the Spanish cultural industries. But it also places those national analyses in an international context by exploring attempts to conquer foreign markets (e.g. Barceló's successful launch on the New York art scene and Ventura

Pons's reinterpretation of US indie cinema) and revealing the varied ways in which producers appeal to categories of 'distinction', often USA-derived, which separate them from the common herd.

For example, Spanish commercial television, long dismissed as trash, has in the last four years opted for a strategy of 'quality' in-house series: high budget, politically progressive and aimed at a select, moneyed demographic. *Periodistas* ('Journalists')*, produced by Berlusconi's Madrid-based network Telecinco and based on US workplace dramas, was the pioneer of this tendency. Likewise, Spanish fashion has concentrated on 'classic' style, an ambiguous category that combines commercial innovation with artistic tradition in such up-market labels as Adolfo Domínguez, whose London stores are located in Regent Street and Covent Garden. During a period when the international art market turned to frivolity, Spain's most celebrated painter, Barceló, opted for 'pure' painting, a high-minded engagement with painterly texture and artistic tradition which he has practised from Paris to Mali. Inversely, Basque artists have shown themselves to be expert in the lingua franca of conceptual art (photography, video, installations), thus achieving a deftly distanced commentary on their own sexual and national conflicts. Meanwhile Ventura Pons has redefined independent cinema in the context of Catalonia: a nation without a state struggling to make its presence felt in the capital-intensive field of feature production. Finally, Almodóvar's most recent films, funded by the French Pathé, achieved cultural distinction to match his box office clout by reworking a form generally considered to be moribund: the 'art movie', with its traditional qualities of formal perfection, thematic seriousness and social prestige. These case histories suggest, ironically perhaps, that cultural innovations may foster commercial success: the contrast with the British film industry's shift down-market into gangster movies, which proved both artistically and financially disastrous, is striking.

Taken together, the six strategies of distinction ('quality', 'classic', 'pure', 'conceptual', 'independent' and 'art') are specific to each medium, yet structurally parallel. And they clearly exemplify Pierre Bourdieu's many analyses of the interrelation of the industrial and the aesthetic in the production of cultural taste. But if Bourdieu is the main theoretical guide here (with his very French analyses adopted and adapted for the different territory of Spain), this book goes beyond the social sphere to examine the aesthetic qualities of cultural objects. After surveying the general state of a medium in its international context and its specific conditions in a national or regional framework, I pay close attention to the particular pleasures of Spanish works. The rhythm and flow of a TV drama, the cut and texture of a T-shirt, the tone and colour of a painting, the layout of a gallery installation, a film sequence shot on location in Barcelona or Madrid – all these are described, analysed and celebrated here.

This new approach requires new research materials. While, as I wrote above, much recent work in cultural studies has been devoted to consumption, I return to production, asking the apparently simple question: how do cultural products come to be made? Vital sources here include the specialized trade press (for all four media of TV, fashion, art and film), which complements or contradicts arts journalism in the general press, and corporate materials. The latter, sometimes supplied to me by the companies themselves, clearly have to be cross-checked with independent sources, but they provide important evidence of corporate culture. While some readers may not be as fascinated as I am by economic aspects of the cultural industries, such knowledge is becoming more widely shared and valued: in Spain, following the UK and USA, weekend movie grosses have migrated from the trade press into the general media. Research on production processes has also been aided by the internet. All the producers I cite here are served by websites, whether their own or those of consumers. The latest news on series drama can be read on www.telecinco.es, and successive seasons of clothing viewed on adolfodominguez.es. A picture search on an engine such as Google will produce an instant gallery of images by the main visual artists treated here, Miquel Barceló and Txomin Badiola. Ventura Pons, Catalan independent, has his own trilingual site, complete with full credits and press notices for each film (venturapons.com). Almodóvar, who has recently launched www.pedroalmodovar.es, is also served by numerous fan sites. Access to Spanish visual culture has thus considerably increased, even as informed understanding of it remains in its infancy.

Three aspects of my critical approach, corresponding once more to the three terms in my title, may be noted at this preliminary point. The first is that, unlike many of those working on contemporary culture who are influenced by the Frankfurt school, I adopt a friendly attitude to my chosen subject, attempting to communicate the excitement I felt in the discovery and the exploration of these diverse objects. Indeed, in the final section of each chapter I address briefly my own experience as a consumer in search of visual pleasure. The second is that, unlike many Leftist critics, particularly in the USA, I stress the local and the particular, as opposed to the global and the universal. Masochistic despair at the supposed dominance of Hollywood sometimes masks a failure to engage with the messy and diverse reality of national and regional audiovisual sectors. Finally, rather than considering culture as an 'exception' to other forms of commerce, as European commentators and regulators often do, I treat it as a privileged form of economic activity. The question I ask with Bourdieu is: how do some cultural objects become endowed with that precious quality known as distinction? Like Bourdieu, again, I attempt to analyse the apparently magical coincidence of individual taste and collective consumption or (to put it in more technical language) of subjective dispositions and objective conditions. However, if aesthetic value is socially created, this does not mean that it is meaningless. Rather, by studying the ways in which visual culture comes into being, circulates and is exchanged, we can appreciate more clearly its unique power and pleasure. Needless to say, I do not myself necessarily endorse the various categories of distinction I treat here: analysis is not to be confused with advocacy.

One advantage of Bourdieu's field theory (in which each work, artist and institution finds meaning only in relation to all the others) is that we no longer need to interrogate cultural texts to see whether they are 'subversive' of the status quo. This critical tic, still frequent in the USA, derives from a simple opposition of hegemony and resistance. While it is clearly fruitless to enquire whether any work of art is 'subversive' in the abstract, Bourdieu side-steps this exhausted debate by refusing to employ such loaded critical terminology. Following his lead, my own empirical research has led me to conclusions which I was not expecting. The main one is that, far from dumbing down, as many Spaniards intuitively believe, much Spanish visual culture has risen in quality. As I note in the final chapter, which cites changes in the demography of cinema audiences in Spain, it is now likely that the financial health of Spanish cinema is dependent on artistic distinction. With the teenage market sewn up by Hollywood, more literate features, appealing to wealthier and better-educated audiences, are a safer bet for a European film industry that has dramatically increased its share of the home market. The 1990s 'upswing' in Spanish audiovisual production, confirmed by the trade press, cannot be explained solely by changes in government subsidy that have encouraged more professional production processes. It also results from a coincidence, apparently magical once more, between the personal and the social, the individual and the collective. As in the case of Spanish television, quality makes money for adventurous and ambitious filmmakers.

While research for the first chapter of this book began in 1998, an update at the time of writing this introduction (January 2002) reveals little change. *Periodistas* remains at the start of its eighth season the most popular drama series on Spanish network television, in spite of many cast changes and a host of imitators. Adolfo Domínguez (current slogan: 'Classic is Avant Garde') continues to consolidate his brand in an economic downturn. Barceló recently exhibited new works on a marine theme (big splashy oils, small sensitive water-colours and bulbous ceramics) at his new Mayfair dealer, Timothy Taylor, while Txomin Badiola, Basque conceptualist, showed at Soledad Lorenzo's prestigious gallery off Madrid's Castellana. Pedro Almodóvar is completing *Hable con ella* ('Speak to Her')*, another female-centred narrative which is said to include a black-and-white sequence recreating early cinema. Most unexpected is Ventura Pons's latest feature, accepted for the 2002 Berlin Festival. Based on David Leavitt's gay-themed novel *The Page Turner*, *The Food of Love* has an English-speaking cast, and is thus Pons's first feature since the no-budget documentary *Ocaña* (1978) not to be made in Catalan.

The question of what constitutes contemporary Spanish (Basque, Catalan or Galician) culture is thus newly problematic, even as national and regional artistic industries show renewed life. Spanish critics universally praised Alejandro Amenábar's masterly horror movie *The Others* (2001) as the most successful 'Spanish' film ever, in spite of the fact that it was made in English. Shot in Cantabria with an all-Spanish crew and a cast headed by Nicole Kidman, *The Others* displays a richly austere aesthetic comparable to the classic fashion I analyse in chapter 2 and held by many to be typically Spanish. But it also reveals as clearly as the six case studies presented in this book that, far from restricting its audience, distinction may serve to enhance the international success of contemporary Spanish culture.

Note

1 See Kinder 1997, Gies 1999, Rodgers 1999, Jordan and Morgan-Tamosunas 2000. My own book *The Moderns* (Smith 2000) addresses a number of media not included in this book (e.g. architecture, popular music, dance) from a variety of perspectives. Two academic journals serve the field: *Arizona Journal of Hispanic Cultural Studies* and *Journal of Spanish Cultural Studies*.

* The author's unofficial translations of titles of works of art appear in roman with quotation marks. Official film titles in English appear in italic.

References

Benton, Lauren A. (1989) Individual Subcontracting and the Informal Sector: The Politics of Restructuring in the Madrid Electronics Industry. In Alejandro Portes, Manuel Castells and Lauren A. Benton (eds), *The Informal Economy: Studies in Advanced and Less Developed Countries*, Baltimore: Johns Hopkins University Press, pp. 228–44.

Gies, David T. (ed.) (1999) *The Cambridge Companion to Modern Spanish Culture*. Cambridge: Cambridge University Press.

Graham, Helen and Labanyi, Jo (eds) (1995) *Spanish Cultural Studies: An Introduction*. Oxford: Oxford University Press.

Jordan, Barry and Morgan-Tamosunas, Rikki (eds) (2000) *Contemporary Spanish Cultural Studies*. London: Arnold.

Kinder, Marsha (ed.) (1997) *Refiguring Spain: Cinema/Media/Representation*. Durham, NC, and London: Duke University Press.

Rodgers, Eamonn (ed.) (1999) *Encyclopedia of Contemporary Spanish Culture*. London: Routledge.

Rosier, Ben (2001) Exportivo La Coruna: Zara Reigns from Spain. *Independent on Sunday* [London], 13 May, Business Section, p. 5.

Smith, Paul Julian (2000) *The Moderns: Time, Space, and Subjectivity in Contemporary Spanish Culture*. Oxford: Oxford University Press.

1 Quality TV? The *Periodistas* Notebook

TV

> I can still not be sure what I took from the whole flow. I believe I registered some incidents as happening in the wrong film, and some characters in the commercials as involved in the film episodes, in what came to seem – for all the occasional bizarre disparities – a single irresponsible flow of images and feelings.
>
> (Williams 1974b: 91–2; cited in Corner 1999: 62)

Like Raymond Williams, recently arrived in Miami and dazzled by the unaccustomed spectacle of US television, the literary or film scholar might be forgiven for disorientation when venturing into TV studies. Stephen Heath has also decried the 'extension, availability, [and] proximity' of television, 'all of which is played out on its screen from show to show in the endless flow' (Heath 1990: 297; quoted in Corner 1999: 69). Whereas a novel or a film is clearly delimited in length, available only from approved agents, and formally separate from the times and spaces of everyday life, the twenty-four hour, domesticated rhythm of television is inseparable from the modern experience it has both reflected and created.

But if television is ubiquitous, it need not be the 'bad machine', endless and irresponsible. Nor do warnings of the globalization of electronic media preclude the emergence of new national programming. In this first chapter, then, I will argue against the sometimes apocalyptic tendencies of some media theory (the philosophical pessimism of 'flow') and for a newly differentiated account of genre, nationality and industrial practice in relation to programme content. As we shall see, some programming sets itself apart from the everyday, and some production companies (even when controlled by multinational conglomerates and operating under the fiercest commercial competition) aim for quality local programming that will attract a select but profitable demographic.

In his excellent synoptic study *Critical Ideas in Television Studies* John Corner (1999) has sought to mediate between social science and the humanities' approaches typified by Williams and Heath above. The latter, he believes, often lack both 'specific analysis of formal structures' and 'detailed engagement with broadcasting history' (69). Corner argues that television must be seen in an institutional context, as an 'ecology' (12) distinct from other mass media such as newspapers (15), not least for the way in which it consistently blurs the boundaries between the public and private spheres. Combining sociologists' concern for 'objectifiable aspects [such as] organization and functioning' with the humanist critics' openness to 'aesthetics, discourse, and value' (10), Corner treats the distinct, but linked, fields of production and reception, pleasure and knowledge, narrative and flow. We can take these fundamental categories in turn.

Production, argues Corner, is relatively neglected in an empirical context, given the difficulty of academic access to a sometimes suspicious media industry (70). Where policy documentation is available (likewise interviews with participants), it raises questions of evidential validity. As a 'moment of multiple intentions' (70), production takes on different usages in TV theory, relating diversely to historical contexts, institutional settings, production mentalities and production practices (71). Questions of both the 'authorial scope' of producers and the 'autonomy', or even 'autism', of institutions (74) are raised most acutely by two forms of programming: news and drama. In both areas empirical enquiry has revealed surprising 'occupational complexity and contingency' and 'complexity of television "authorship"' (76–7), even when select 'quality' programming is produced by a company with distinctive audience demographics, corporate history and socio-aesthetic profile (78).

The sociologically tinged concept of production is, however, inseparable from the interest in reception that was spearheaded by the humanities, and most particularly by cultural studies (80). For reception is also multiple and contingent, occurring at the intersection of social and psychological needs and having unintended consequences (82). And while some scholars see reception as reproducing 'structured social inequalit[ies]' (84), others, of the 'uses and gratifications' school (85), stress not the pernicious effects of the

medium on public communication but rather the 'cultural competence' of the viewer, most especially of drama (86). More particularly,
recent changes in 'multiple consumption opportunities' have seen a
change in programme address: from the 'ideologies of the home
to . . . individualized commodity taste' (90).

The newer focus on gratification and taste has arisen out of attempts to study the elusive topic of television pleasure, once more an
emphasis of cultural studies. If television, unlike cinema, is universally required to provide both public information and entertainment,
then critics read the pleasure it provides either negatively, as a form
of 'cultural debasement' (93), or positively, as a challenge to elite,
high culture (94). TV pleasures are visual, parasocial or dramatic.
They may be based on new knowledge, comedy or fantasy, or (altern-
atively) on the familiar notions of distraction, diversion and routine
(99). The debate around 'quality' to which I return later is also riven
by 'a tension between publicly protected cultural values and the
popular pleasures of cultural markets' (107).

If pleasure is critically debated, knowledge is no less problematic.
Corner rehearses 'three types of badness' often attributed to television:
mis-selection (in which the TV 'gatekeeper' rules out inadmissible
content); misrepresentation (in which the imagistic brevity and
narrativization of TV form traduce the complexity of the real); and
mis-knowing (in which the perceptual or cognitive aspects of the
knowledge process itself are debased) (109–10). The move from print
to electronic media is thus seen as a decline: from ideas to feeling,
appearance and mood; or from 'Is it true? Is it false?' to 'How does
it look? How does it feel?' (113). Conversely, commentators have
seen the extension of public knowledge through broadcasting as the
'democratization of everyday life' and the creation of a 'mediated
democratic polity' (114) impossible through print.

Crucial to Corner here is the question of drama. The emotional
engagement generated by fiction, and most particularly by workplace dramas, 'informs social understanding' in such areas as occu-
pation, family, health and money (115). Narrative, then (even in the
infinite form of soap opera), can perhaps be read as a final antidote
to flow theory. For although the incursion of narrative into TV
journalism (where segments have long been known as 'stories') has
been read as an 'erosion' (47) of the informational and expository
values of the medium, both spoken and enacted narrative constitute
a 'significant dimension of modern public knowledge' (59). The
depth of virtual relationship enjoyed by viewers with the characters
of series drama ('the sense of coexistence between real and fictive
worlds' (59)) thus forms a distinctive socio-aesthetic profile that is

worthy of analysis, and is not to be dismissed as the narcotic alienation of a 'dramatized society' (Corner 1999: 48, citing Williams
1974a).

Quality TV

> Quality makes money.
>
>> (Grant Tinker, President MTM;
>> cited Feuer, Kerr, and Vahimagi 1984: 26)

Corner highlights the conflict in debates on quality between institutions and aesthetics. On the one hand, ' "quality" signals a concern
with defining more clearly what . . . can be assessed as a good product and thereby used as a marker in both public and corporate
audits of the industry' (106). This objectifiable dimension, derived
from management theory and relating to such areas as corporate
restructuring and industrial standards, slips, on the other hand, into
more subjective notions: 'questions of generic preference, class, gender and age-related variations in cultural taste, and different ways of
relating to the popular' (106). As so often, it is in drama and entertainment that such issues are raised most acutely.

Other scholars further complexify this schema. Geoff Mulgan
(1990) cites no fewer than seven types of quality, of which only the
first two are dealt with by Corner: producer quality and professionalism (8), consumer quality and the market (10), quality and the
medium: television's aesthetic (15), television as ritual and commu-
nion (19), television and the person (21), the televisual ecology (24)
and, finally, quality as diversity (26). Most commentators, however,
line up on one side of the divide between production and reception.
John Thornton Caldwell (1994) sees the producers' need for what
he variably calls 'loss leader', 'event status' and 'special' programming (162–3), which undercuts three cherished beliefs of media
theorists: namely, the supposed populism, mundaneness and bound-
lessness of televisual flow (163). On the contrary, writes Caldwell,
'loss-leader events programmes make every effort to underscore and
illuminate their textual borders,' making the 'bounds of distinction
. . . a crucial part of the genre' (163). Kim Christian Schrøder (1992),
on the other hand, attempts to pin down the 'phantom' of cultural
quality by offering a 'reception perspective on cultural value' (199).
Following Bourdieu's lead on the role of distinction in conferring
'aesthetic status on objects that are banal or even "common" ' (199),

Schrøder rejects the elitism and paternalism implicit in both British and American television culture (200), arguing that 'quality' can only exist as 'quality for someone' (211). He further proposes that for certain audiences popular series drama does indeed trigger the ethical and aesthetic values traditionally attributed to art, while engaging a third dimension: an 'ecstatic' realm of release and loss of control (213).

Schrøder's is a position piece which does not engage closely with particular programmes, aiming rather to 'open a discussion' on populism and diversity (215). But he does challenge the specific corporate study responsible for introducing the quality debate into academic TV studies: *MTM: 'Quality Television'*, by Feuer, Kerr and Vahimagi (1984). 'This new addition to critical discussion is not occasioned by a general re-evaluation of the products of the cultural industry,' writes Schrøder, 'but by a handful of outstanding programmes (notably *Hill Street Blues*) from one unique production company (MTM) which function almost as the exception that proves the rule of commercial American television. By labelling MTM programmes "at once artistic and industrial" . . . the analysis clearly presupposes a frame of understanding in which the artistic is almost by nature at odds with the industrial' (201).

If we turn to Feuer et al.'s study, however, we discover that this is by no means the case, for these authors consistently relate institution and aesthetics, industry and art. Thus the 'MTM style' is inseparable from factors that are both material and formal: shooting on film rather than video tape, employing actors schooled in new improvisational techniques, offering creative staff an unusual amount of freedom (32). A specialist 'indie prod', MTM was both exceptional (in fulfilling the distinctive criteria for televisual 'authorship') and typical (in being subject to the same commercial laws of ratings and cancellation as the rest of the industry) (33). In spite or because of these commercial constraints (which fostered a demand for both repetition of the old and innovation of the new), MTM marked off the boundaries between it and the mainstream producers in both content and form: highlighting sensitive topical issues (140), blurring the genres of comedy and drama (149), and changing the look and sound of prime time with hand-held camera and overlapping sound (148). *Hill Street Blues*, MTM's most celebrated workplace drama, thus emerged out of 'a complex intersection of forces in late 1970s American television [including] NBC's short lived but decisive strategy to sidestep Nielsen aggregates [i.e. brute numbers of viewers] by buying "high quality" consumers via "quality" programmes' (150).

MTM's industrial context is thus as complex and overdetermined as the artistic texture of its programming with its dense construction, dexterous orchestration of tone, panoramic points of view, and intricate, yet integrated, story lines (151). *Hill Street* was as difficult to police for the jittery network, fearful of offending sponsors, as it was for media academics, anxious to pin down its ambiguous liberal politics in a time of reaction. What seems clear, however, is that the series offered select viewers new and challenging forms of pleasure and knowledge, and that the corporate study of MTM gives the lie to media academics who view 'quality' as the cynical underscoring of phantom bounds of distinction.

Spanish TV

Except for the occasional strip show or pornographic film, the programming of all [Spanish] channels is very similar to American broadcast television (not to mention the dominance of U.S. products as a percentage of all telefilms, series, and feature films broadcast). . . . The quality varies as much as in any broadcast system, and like most national media industries everywhere, the various Spanish TV channels repulse and attract on a pretty even score across their audiences.

(Maxwell 1995: p. xxiv)

There would appear to be few territories less promising for quality television, however defined, and more hospitable to the philosophical pessimism of 'flow' than Spain. Anecdotally, literate Spaniards dismiss their television system as the 'teletonta' or 'telebasura'. Domestic and foreign journalists reconfirm the stereotype, citing the 'incessant controversy' around the corruption and bias of state television (*El País* 1999) and the crass appeal to sex in the ratings war unleashed by commercial networks such as Telecinco and Antena 3 (Hooper 1995: 317). One Spanish academic stresses the defencelessness of Spain in the global marketplace, lacking as it does a 'national champion to defend [its] colours' (Bustamante 1995: 361); one Briton laments the lack of 'an effective method of regulating programme output [and of] redefin[ing] the notion of public service in relation to the more complex multi-channel and multi-media situation' (Jordan 1995: 368).

The most distinguished scholar of Spanish television, Richard Maxwell (1995), offers a near-apocalyptic institutional history. Maxwell stresses the suddenness of change in Spain: 'In a little more than fifteen years, Spanish television made the transition from absolute state control to a regulated competitive system of national and regional networks of mixed private and public ownership' (p. xxiv).[1] Maxwell's narrative is one of relentless decline: from 'the death of the Dictator and the twilight of national mass media' (3), through the 'crisis' associated with the Rightist UCD (40), to the 'diminishing returns' of the Socialists' modernizing corporatism (72). He concludes: 'No longer fit for a nation, except on paper, national mass media have been absorbed into processes of privatization of communication around the world, and Spain has just been one more stomping ground of this global juggernaut' (153–4).

Less dramatically, Maxwell analyses here (1995) and later (1997) the legislation specific to Spain which apparently contributed to such general effects: the Statute of [State] Radio and Television of 1980, which redefined the role of RTVE; the Third Channel Law of 1984, which regulated regional broadcasting; and the Private TV Law of 1988, which gave birth to Antena 3, Telecinco and Canal Plus (Maxwell 1997: 261–2). Linking this local legislation to the global juggernaut are Maxwell's three 'salient issues': 'privatization, globalization (or transnationalization), and regionalization (or decentralization)' (1995: p. xxv). The Spanish media experience is 'illuminating', writes Maxwell, 'because of the clearly defined bonds and collisions among regional, national, and transnational media spaces' (p. xxv).

Maxwell is not concerned with programme content; and it comes as some surprise to read in a footnote that he takes pleasure in Spanish television: 'The absence of hierarchical judgments or elitist frameworks [in this study] to inform readers of Spanish media talents is intentional. That I like Spanish TV is irrelevant. Its worth is a question of taste, tradition, closed markets, and cultural translation' (1995: 156, n. 9). What is curious here is how US media theorists are so fascinated by globalization that they fail to engage with the distinctively national content of programming.[2] Indeed, as we shall see, Spain may even speak back to US producers, modulating, however slightly, the route of the juggernaut through transnational space. Such subjective matters as 'questions of taste and tradition' (of reception and pleasure) clearly merit equal attention to that accorded objectively verifiable standards of production and knowledge. Certainly Spanish programmes deserve academic consideration comparable to that granted their equivalents in the UK and USA. Developments since Maxwell's pioneering studies suggest that, far from being dominated by North American programming, domestic production of comedy and drama has proved crucial to the survival of the multinationals in Spain; and a recent 'territory guide' in one of the media trade journals also gives a more nuanced perspective than the global view of academic theory. *Television Business International* devoted a special issue to 'Spanish TV's New Challenges' in June 1997. On the eve of the launch of two competing digital platforms, *TBI* asks whether the heavily indebted broadcast sector is ready for yet more channels, and when the new Partido Popular government will implement the EE directive's quotas on independent production (17). The state RTVE remains 'the sick man of Spanish TV' (18), with audience share falling from 43 per cent in 1991 to 26.9 per cent in 1996 (19), while free-to-air 'private net[work]s Antena 3 and Telecinco are neck-and-neck in audience share' (20). Pay TV Canal Plus is also 'one of the success stories of the 1990s' (24), in spite of tax increases imposed by a new government on a company closely linked with the previous Socialist regime (25). Likewise, the 'local heroes' serving six independent regions are 'living through good times', with audience share growing in prime time to 19 per cent, the highest peak since the arrival of private television in 1990 (26). Finally, domestic production has experienced a relative 'boom' with 'home produced fiction . . . well received on television, beating all the American product' (29).

Such commercial surveys not only are at odds with academic pessimism; they also provide almost the only data on programme content, noting such trends as the 'diversification into dramas and sitcoms, [which] creat[es] hits like . . . *Médico de familia* (*Family Doctor*), which pulls in shares of over 50 per cent on Telecinco' (29). The pleasures of such domestic narratives, clearly central to public entertainment and information in Spain, deserve a sympathetic and informed analysis in both their institutional and artistic aspects, an analysis that they have yet to receive.

Telecinco

Telecinco firmly believes in the free competition that characterizes a true market and in profitability as the only business strategy.
(Telecinco 1999a: 'Telecinco hoy: introducción')[3]

If ever there was a candidate for television as 'bad machine', it would appear to be Telecinco. It was Telecinco that pushed the envelope for sex programming at the start of the 1990s with the notorious stripping game show *¡Uf, qué calor!*. With a shifting team of majority foreign stockholders that evaded Spanish legislation and includes Berlusconi's Fininvest, it is also exemplary of Maxwell's privatized, globalized juggernaut. Detailed engagement with broadcasting history, however (not to mention formal analysis of programme content), points to a different and more complex story, one in which, paradoxically perhaps, loss of ratings led to an increase in innovative, in-house production.

Brief reports in the trade press document the chequered history of Telecinco. In 1990 'Telecinco['s] launch [was] under threat' (Grabsky 1990), with the future of the nascent company in jeopardy after a boardroom struggle between publishing group Anaya, which favoured news and cultural programming, and Berlusconi and ONCE (Spain's national organization for the blind), which preferred movies and mini-series. By 1994, when strip, game and reality shows had lost their novelty value, *Cineinforme* reported (Anon. 1994) that Telecinco was 'in search of a new identity', attempting to correct a loss of share through a new programming policy that emphasized original programming. By 1996 share had increased by two points to 21.5 per cent of national viewing, and Spanish publishing group Correo increased its stake (Scott 1996). The year 1997 saw reports both that Berlusconi and his brother faced fraud charges over management of Gestevisión, a subsidiary of Telecinco, in 1991–3 (del Valle 1997) and that 'Telecinco plans expansion into the Americas' (Green 1997), capitalizing on in-house productions that were now 'the most popular in Spain'. Finally, in 1998, the Supreme Court ruled that the granting of private TV licences by the Spanish government in 1989 (to Canal Plus and Gestevisión-Telecinco), which remained controversial, was indeed lawful (Pérez Gómez 1998).

Once more it is *Television Business International* that gives the fullest account of Telecinco's 'turn around', based as it is on two aspects of managerial 'quality': corporate restructuring and industrial standards (*TBI* 1997). After aggressive competition for audience share with rival private web Antena 3 had led to falling ratings and mushrooming debt, Maurizio Carlotti was brought in from Italy by Fininvest as director general in 1994 (22). Attacking the 'financial chaos rampant in the Spanish television sector', Carlotti rapidly reduced debt and cut staff, announcing that Telecinco 'would no longer compete to be an audience leader'. Relieved of this burden and with a modest target share of 18–21 per cent, 'paradoxically', writes *TBI*, '[Telecinco has been] allowed to take the lead' with distinctive new formats including satirical gossip shows, mixes of news and humour, and Letterman-style talk (23). Key, however, is fiction production, with Telecinco's own studios nicknamed 'the

Fiction Factory' and substantial investment committed to feature films and expansion to the Americas (23). Such industrial and cosmetic changes (a new logo and design) are 'aimed especially at promoting a youthful, fashionable image to attract the more middle class audience that Telecinco is increasingly directed toward'.

Like NBC in the 1970s, then, Telecinco sought, temporarily at least, a select demographic (young, wealthy and urban) in the belief that quality could make more money than the *telebasura* for which they were once notorious. And by looking at Telecinco's own policy documentation, we can move, as Corner recommends, from historical contexts and institutional settings to production mentalities and practices. We will also be able to analyse one crucial aspect of managerial quality: 'delivery of schedules in line with stated company policy' (Corner 1999: 106).

Unsurprisingly, Telecinco's own account coincides with the 'turn around' narrative of the trade press (Telecinco 1999a). The introduction to the first section of its website ('Telecinco Today') claims that the Spanish TV market has matured and that Telecinco is known for both its profitability and its innovative programming. 'Professional management' has led to leadership in its target audience ('between 15–54, middle, upper middle and upper class, in towns bigger than 10,000 inhabitants'). The website lays particular emphasis on news programming, based on innovative Digital Editing technology. While state TVE is still ahead for individual bulletins, Telecinco claims to lead in total hours of news ('Telecinco hoy: programación y audiencia').

The account of shareholders and management structure stresses (against popular conception) the 'national and international' make-up of the group: Italian Mediaset (holding company for Fininvest), German producer and distributor Kirch, Spanish multimedia Correo and publisher Planeta ('Accionariado y organigrama'). The description of the Telecinco Group stresses its multimedia holdings, including advertising, news, music, multiplexes and the Picasso Studios ('largest fiction producer in Spain'), and claims that economies of scale have now made Telecinco one of the most profitable channels in Europe.

Significantly, Telecinco claims to combine public values with private markets. The 'independence and credibility' of its news service is one of the 'pillars' of the group ('Informativos Telecinco'); the other is original production. Telecinco promotes its prize-winning talk shows (with live programming a specialty), as it does its in-house drama: 'Original production in series drama is one of the distinguishing features of the chain. Currently Telecinco, through its producer

Estudios Picasso, has many hits including *Médico de familia*, [and] *Periodistas* (*Journalists*)' (1999a: 'Programación'). Such series benefit from their own 'particular style', and are 'intended to satisfy all kinds of audience'. It is in the section on acquisitions and co-productions that the word 'quality', implicit throughout, explicitly appears. 'Cult' US drama imports (*Murder One, Ally McBeal*) are also a key characteristic of the channel's programming. It is perhaps no accident that such quality, issue-driven content is directly followed by Telecinco's mission statement of social service: the web is committed to the environment, to social solidarity, and to the audiovisual education of children, a concern for public values shown by its provision of a telephone information service and its increase in subtitled provision for the deaf, as recommended by the Ministry of Culture ('Al servicio de la sociedad').

It would be naive to take such self-presentation without a grain of salt, although the objective data on renewed profitability and innovative programming coincide with the external sources of the trade press. The value of this policy documentation, however, is as evidence of the interplay between institutional settings and production mentalities, between organization and aesthetics. Devoted to profitability and controlled by foreign interests, Telecinco nevertheless sees fit to risk the ratings for a moment, and court viewers with quality domestic drama.

Periodistas: series concept

Telecinco Launches New Newspaper

Tuesday, 13 January 1998
At 9.30 p.m. Telecinco gives birth to 'Crónica Universal', a weekly newspaper featuring great actors every Tuesday night. Amparo Larrañaga, Belén Rueda, and José Coronado, together with a prestigious cast of 15 fixed characters, play the protagonists in the highly crafted episodes that go to make up the series *Periodistas*. A workplace comedy with dramatic elements, this series represents an important step forward compared to previous series, enjoying as it does significantly higher production values.

(Telecinco 1998b: 1)

The production mentality behind the *Periodistas* concept is revealed by the glossy Telecinco annual report for 1998 (Telecinco 1998a).

Under its four watchwords of 'innovation, independence, quality, and profitability' (17), Telecinco promotes its 'first Fiction Factory', the Picasso Studios, which produce 400 hours a year with an average of ten projects being shot simultaneously (24). 'Quality Fiction' boasts 'new narrative structures' (43), including an action series set in a police station, the first series shot wholly in a national park ('lobbying for the defence of the environment'), an all-female drama and, finally, the first sitcoms and suspense dramas to 'reproduce North American production systems' (43). Within this slate, Telecinco's two crown jewels are *Médico de familia* (with the highest ratings of any programme since the introduction of private TV) and *Periodistas*, distinguished by its workplace setting and topical subject matter (40).

Even more revealing, however, are the publicity materials produced by Telecinco's press office, and thus unseen by *Periodistas*' prospective audience. The first press kit came in newspaper form (Telecinco 1998b).[4] Claiming that the series sought to give 'the more human face of journalists', it featured the back stories of no fewer than eighteen characters. The 'luxury cast' (2) is headed by Luis (José Coronado),

1 *Periodistas*: the ensemble cast of the first season, including Laura (Amparo Larrañaga) and Luis (José Coronado), front row, centre. Courtesy of Telecinco.

a New York correspondent separated from his wife who returns to Spain as head of local news, and Laura (Amparo Larrañaga), a single woman dedicated to her career who is promoted to deputy editor, and thus becomes Luis's immediate boss. Interviews with Daniel Écija, director and executive producer, and Mikel Lejarza, Vice-President of Content at Telecinco, reveal an unstable combination of novelty and tradition in the concept. Écija states that 'We want to push the envelope, not to burst it', while Lejarza claims that 'At Telecinco we like to innovate', but admits that a similar US series would have five times the budget (3). Elsewhere claims are less modest: we are informed that this is the first series in Spain set in a journalistic milieu, and that it draws on 'classic [newsroom] pioneers' such as MTM's *Mary Tyler Moore Show* and *Lou Grant* (4); or again, we are told that '*Periodistas* inaugurates a new TV genre', whose main characteristics are a risky shift to the professional arena, away from those 'domestic problems with which the audience can easily identify'. Other novel features include the ensemble cast (both veteran and novice), the high-quality scripts (team-written and co-ordinated), and the exterior sequences, permitted by a relatively high budget.

In a second 'issue' of the mock newspaper sent to journalists on 14 September 1998, the press office gave figures for the first season. Telecinco's gamble had paid off, with an average share of 26.6 per cent and 4,700,000 audience (Telecinco 1998c: 1). It also scored the highest numbers in the most sought-after demographic (given here as '25–44'), an audience which enjoyed its 'new young brand of humour, with a more acid and ironic tone'. Chiming here with the sophisticated, youthful and often female target audience are the novel domestic set-ups: households comprising a divorcé and daughter, male friends, female friends, a separated woman and her child, an unmarried couple, and a single woman and her mother. Issues raised by the second season include the neglect of the elderly, nuclear pollution and the destructive potential of religious sects (1). A follow-up interview with executive Lejarza has him stressing that the first season's episodes on euthanasia, squatting and domestic violence had 'anticipated' the news (2). Moreover, introducing a 'cinema effect' on television, *Periodistas* has enjoyed the 'best image quality' and become the 'best quality series drama' on television (2).

Figures reveal the considerable investment in both financial and human resources required to achieve this goal: after twenty-one episodes the series had used 180 actors, employing 110 people in the production of each episode. And, spurning the sofas and kitchens

2 *Periodistas*: exterior shooting in Madrid, with Blas (Alex Ángulo, left) and José Antonio (Pepón Nieto). Courtesy of Telecinco.

of domestic drama familiar on Spanish TV, it devoted at least two days per episode to location shooting in an often uncooperative Madrid. Of the remaining scenes, 44 per cent are shot in the press room, and 11 per cent in the bar in which the characters socialize, with the home sets of the two principal characters accounting for just 4 and 5 per cent of scenes.

As ratings soared to a peak of over 6 million viewers on 20 April 1999, and the series was sold to Portugal and Italy, it seemed that Telecinco's quest for profit through quality was assured. The hybrid comedy-drama of *Periodistas* trounced prime-time competitors, whether US feature films or domestic drama starring such prestigious film stars as Carmen Maura and Jorge Sanz.[5] Moreover, moving to Monday at 9.50 p.m. (Spanish prime time), *Periodistas* was flanked by two more of the successful generic hybrids for which Telecinco was well known: *El Informal* (news and humour) and *Crónicas Marcianas* (Letterman-style chat and comedy). The schedule was thus in line with stated policy objectives, and delivered the required audience: *Periodistas* has been sponsored by a luxury watch brand, and major advertisers include a high proportion of designer fragrance, cosmetic and hair care products.

Market forces, however, do not exclude social responsibility. Indeed, the series addresses precisely those areas cited in Telecinco's mission statement: the environment (e.g. food safety), solidarity with minorities (prisoners, the homeless, the disabled), and children (child abuse). And with Telecinco's distinctive profile based as much on its news operation as on its original drama, the series fused these two 'pillars'. In a reflexive gesture typical of MTM's quality drama, it thus incorporated the debate over informational independence and authority into its characteristic plots. Indeed, the fact that the drama anticipated the news (with an episode on euthanasia preceding a real-life drama on the same theme by just days) lent *Periodistas* added expository value, routinely denied news programmes criticized for being overly dependent on narrative. Executive Lejarza claims that television is not good or bad, only up to date or out of date (Telecinco 1998c: 2). The apparently uncanny topicality of *Periodistas* testifies to its closeness to Spanish audiences, a closeness that reflects their national tastes and traditions more pleasurably (and profitably) than rival and lower-rated transnational production: in a typical week (22–28 March 1999) *Periodistas* stood at second place in the charts (after a national football match), while Schwarzenegger's *The Last Action Hero* was at nine and Telecinco's prize import *Ally McBeal* at ten.[6]

The Telecinco website has featured a group photo of the cast of *Periodistas* inviting viewers to participate in an on-line activity: sending the picture and autograph greetings of your favourite star to a friend by e-mail. This is unusually explicit evidence for the parasocial function of TV stars as intermediaries between viewers, evidence that can also be gleaned from press coverage. The press clippings for March 1999 (some 200 pages in length) focus either on public manifestations of the quality of the series (the award of prestigious prizes to its actors, including one from the readers of respected film periodical *Fotogramas*) or on gossip about their private lives (paparazzi shots in magazines such as *Interviú* which blur the divide between real and fictional partners and pregnancies) (Telecinco 1999b). Such coverage reveals the erosion of informational values which Corner had suggested is typical of TV 'stories', whether news or drama. But it seems clear that *Periodistas* has succeeded in its attempt to blend social understanding and emotional engagement in a way that counts as 'quality' for an audience as diverse as movie buffs and gossip addicts. And focusing as it does on the news production process (making explicit the 'goalkeeper' function of the media), the series overtly poses the journalistic questions 'Is it true? Is it false?' typical

3 *Periodistas*: the newsroom set, with Willy (Joel Joan, third from right)
and Ali (Esther Arroyo, far right). Courtesy of Telecinco.

of print culture, even as it asks the 'How does it feel?' and shows us
the 'How does it look?' typical of the electronic media.

Is there, then, a 'Telecinco style', analogous to the 'MTV style'?
While Telecinco is hardly an 'indie prod', and its executives prefer
not to make comparisons with US product, *Periodistas* is, in fact,
strikingly similar in form to the pioneering North American workplace
dramas and sitcoms. The topicality, generic fusion and technical
innovation are comparable; the development and delayed resolution
of deep and surface plot lines, the 'rounding' of characters through
unexpected facets, and the shifts in tone from comedy to pathos, all
are familiar. More precisely, the muted piano and wind theme tune
cites *Hill Street Blues* as clearly as the morning meeting which begins
each episode and re-establishes the ensemble cast for the viewer.
But perhaps the clearest sign of *Periodistas* novelty in Spain is an
aspect that diverges from the US models. While North American
titles are typically enigmatic or laconic (*Hill Street Blues*, *LA Law*,
ER), the Spanish title is terse but unambiguous. Unfamiliar with
the workplace format in domestic product, Spanish audiences were
perhaps felt to need more explicit framing in order to prepare themselves for Telecinco's relatively risky venture.

Periodistas: specimen episode

Episode 28 (21 December 1998)

'Dos con leche y uno solo'[7]
Grandfather Manolo and his friend Matías (from *Médico de familia*)
appear in the press room of *Crónica Universal*. The reason for their visit
is that they have found a finger in a tin of food and decide to use their
friendship with Herminio, the caretaker at the newspaper, to get publicity for their misadventure. At first no one takes them seriously but Luis
then insists José Antonio take up their case. Laura is feeling unwell.
Mamen advises her to get a check up, but Laura has been prudent and
has already had tests. To surprise all round, the results show she is
pregnant. Willy and Clara do a report on how winning the lottery can
change your life. In order to illustrate the story, they interview a middle
aged woman who became a millionaire a year ago thanks to the lottery.
This woman will try to win over Willy's affections, awakening strange
reactions in Clara. Blas is not coping well with his separation from Mamen,
especially in this festive season. He is so upset that he winds up getting
drunk at the office Christmas party. Mamen, for her part, feels guilty at
having caused this situation.

(Telecinco 1998d)

This Christmas episode of *Periodistas* is perhaps atypical of the series
as a whole, lacking both topicality and the hard issues for which the
drama is known. However, the guest appearance by members of
Telecinco's other hit *Médico de familia*, typical of special 'event' programming for the holidays, is not simply an example of gratuitous
cross-promotion, but rather raises important questions of cultural
taste and audience profile central to *Periodistas'* production and reception. More characteristically, the social issues that are raised are
immediately personalized: the plot line of the finger found in the
tin of (archetypal) chickpeas is here treated humorously, shown as
it is from the point of view of the elderly characters familiar to
audiences from the other show. (In other episodes, nuclear contam-
ination, say, will be presented with proper seriousness.) And the
journalistic 'story' on the social effects of the lottery becomes regular character Willy's attempted seduction by an attractive, independent middle-aged winner who appears only in this episode.
Typical, however, of the screenwriters' avoidance of cliché is that
the latter has not been adversely affected by her sudden wealth, but
rather has taken pleasure in and advantage of it, seeing young, sexy
Willy (the programme's inveterate Don Juan) as yet another promising acquisition.

The pre-credit sequence, set in Luis's kitchen at breakfast time, introduces this continuing theme of comic or ironic reversal of sex and age roles. With typical overlapping dialogue, Luis argues loudly with Blas (prize-winning Basque film actor Alex Ángulo) about how to use the toaster. Deftly and silently, Luis's teenage daughter solves their problem. The tone is subtly modulated here. Blas is recently separated from wife Mamen, hence his presence in Luis's flat, typical of the casual and consensual households in a series which features not one married couple with children. And when Blas battles with the toaster, moaning 'I don't understand it', he is clearly also referring to his marital problems, which will trace a narrative arc in the following hour.

This episode, which credits three directors and scriptwriters,[8] features eleven locations and some twenty-seven segments, of which seven are shot as exteriors. The latter amount to only ten minutes in all (the same as the single establishing sequence in the newsroom), and are frequently unmotivated by the plot. When Laura and Mamen discuss Christmas preparations while strolling in a shopping mall, the effect is topical, given the time of year, but hardly dramatic. Such exteriors seem intended to reinforce the quality 'look' and reputation which Telecinco's press agency promoted so vigorously. Conversely, a late sequence shot in the crowded pedestrian shopping areas south of Madrid's Gran Vía provides a moment of what Schrøder calls 'ecstatic' release from the everyday (1992: 213). Blas spots Mamen in the crowd and, as they embrace, reconciled, the camera first circles around them before soaring above the festive shoppers in a rare crane shot.

In interiors the main technical innovation is the steadycam. The sinuous unbroken takes (reminiscent of a less frenetic *ER*) are used to disorientating effect in the post-credit newsroom sequence, where we follow the elderly visitors through the bustling, cluttered set, as they are fobbed off by each of the regular characters in turn. The public space of the open-plan newsroom, subdivided into the semi-private spaces of kitchen and bosses' offices, serves, like the other recurring location of the downstairs bar, to facilitate the interconnection of the various personal and professional relationships. Not only do Luis and Laura, Blas and Mamen, Willy and Clara (three couples displaying distinct forms of conflict) share the same spaces; they are typically joined by camera movement (panning or tracking shots) which fluidly links one piece of dialogue to the next. In a very wordy episode, with none of the set-piece action sequences on which the series prides itself (an explosion in a service station, a car pitching into a reservoir), same sex discussions, marking solidarity and friendship, alternate with opposite sex arguments, reflecting both desire and distrust. Typically, however, when pregnant boss Laura gives deserted secretary Mamen a sisterly hug, the 'warm moment'[9] is ironically undercut by Mamen's wary reaction: career woman Laura has not previously been known for offering emotional support.

The mix of comedy and pathos is characteristically combined with deep-level plot lines that remain unresolved and surface stories concluded by the end of the hour. The main example of the former is the sexual and professional tension between Luis and Laura, central to the concept as described in Telecinco's initial press kit, which cites the premiss of US comedy-drama of the 1980s *Moonlighting* (Telecinco 1998b: 2). When, in the first half, Luis chooses to commit to Laura, she rejects his attempt to take over her life and considers abortion; when she decides to commit to him at the end, he rejects her in turn, having just learned that he has also impregnated the wife from whom he is separated. Surface stories include the comic subplot of the severed finger (whose origin is revealed at the end) and the seduction of the great seducer Willy (who finally rejects his protector's tempting offer). As in all quality drama series, continuing narrative threads are used to lend regular characters unexpected traits and thus render them 'round': the sexy, superficial and impoverished Willy was hardly likely to reject a wealthy patron, as he does; Luis, a paragon of professional ethics, is, as his young daughter reminds him in a comic reversal, unforgivably careless in his private life; ambitious Laura, who has always resisted her mother's advice to marry and have kids, suddenly sees the attractions of maternity. In this female-led character comedy, plot, psychology and tone are interdependent.

When Laura complains to Mamen that men are a different species to women, she ruefully qualifies this: men are the inferior species. Flattering the female audience with a gallery of attractive and active urban women, *Periodistas* also courts youth. Laura's mother (the only older person in the regular cast) is impossible; the elderly visitors are patronized by the journalists (and audience) even as they complain of discrimination on the basis of age, the kind of issue taken seriously in other episodes. More importantly, this episode appeals to a distinctive cultural context that contradicts Maxwell's assertion that a globalized Spanish TV is 'no longer fit for a nation' (1995: 153). The episode is dense with references to specifically Spanish practices associated with the festive season and variably integrated into the plot lines: the lottery (whose singing children are imitated by the office clown), Mamen's purchase of too much *turrón* in the shopping mall (the sign of her personal problems), the grapes of

New Year's Eve, and the gifts of *Reyes*. Arguably the most distinctively national element, however, is the language itself, with its multiple registers and references. The episode title 'Dos con leche y uno solo' thus features an untranslatable pun. Apparently referring to 'Two white [coffees] and one black', the double pregnancy plot reveals it to mean 'Two inseminated [women] and one solitary man'. Condemned to lose in translation the idiomatic ambiguity of US titles (as in the pallid Spanish version *Canción triste de Hill Street*), domestic drama here exploits a peculiarly Spanish tolerance for obscenity that would be inadmissible on the US networks.

Fit for the *estado de las autonomías*, *Periodistas* makes little of its Madrid location, and takes care to include representatives in its choral cast of the historic nationalities and regions: Mamen is Galician, while trainee José Ramón and gossip columnist Ali are Andalusian. But *Periodistas* also acknowledges that an awareness of cosmopolitan culture is part of the Spanish urban life-style that the series both reflects and fosters. A visit to a sushi bar or a bookstore-cum-cafe are everyday occurrences in *Periodistas* not likely to be available to viewers in Albacete. Satirical colleagues compare Willy to Richard Gere in *American Gigolo* ('He started with silk shirts and ended up a Buddhist'), while sophisticated Ali compares the noisy antics of the *Médico de familia* household to US prime-time soap of the 1980s *Falcon Crest*.

What Maxwell calls the 'bonds between regional, national, and transnational media spaces' (Maxwell 1995: p. xxv) are played out in such dialogue. But the festive incursion of Telecinco's most popular comedy into its most prestigious drama raises questions of cultural taste and competing definitions of quality repressed by a normal episode. Sitting on the domestic sofa and eating lentils in the family kitchen (precisely those locations that the *Periodistas'* concept sought to avoid), José Ramón and Ali can barely conceal their distaste. Broadly acted, crudely stereotypical, and unapologetically domestic and everyday, *Médico de familia* represents another, older appeal to 'the popular' by the same channel and studio. Ideologically ambiguous (difficult to 'police'), *Periodistas* here both underscores the textual borders between its self and its other (between cosmopolitan sushi and parochial lentils) and incorporates that earlier cultural profile into its own broad framework. This incorporation is quite literal: in an atypically farcical moment José Ramón believes that he has ingested the missing finger along with the lentils he has so greedily consumed in the family kitchen. Poised once more between repetition and innovation, *Periodistas* dare not desert a mass prime-time audience even as it addresses itself to the quality demographic.

Stop the Press

A night spent viewing Telecinco leaves the British spectator as disorientated by the integrated 'flow' of images as Raymond Williams was in Miami. The presenters of satirical gossip show *El Informal* promote *Periodistas* within their own programme; a split-screen display combines the names and logos of the sponsor (spokesperson Antonio Banderas), network and programme; and the one-minute, pre-credit sequence is followed by a full seven minutes of commercials and promos (including a preview of the late night talk show *Crónicas Marcianas* that will follow *Periodistas*). This is the first of three extended breaks which will take the sixty minutes of drama to the scheduled hour and a half. Given this constant interruption, it is perhaps unsurprising that Telecinco's much-trumpeted lead on Monday nights (all three shows are number one in their respective time slots) disguises fluctuations in viewer attention documented by independent figures: *Periodistas'* 'peak' audience and share, however, are attested to at 11.40 p.m. on 19 April 1999 with an astonishing 7,900,000 viewers and 51 per cent (Telecinco 1999c (unpaginated)).

If this 'blocking' of key shows on a single evening of 'must-see TV' is reminiscent of US network scheduling, the late hour of peak viewing is a reminder of the distinctively national profile of Spanish domestic rhythms, alien indeed to US definitions of prime time. Yet we have seen that each of the terms I have used in this chapter is problematic. 'Spanish' television is, as Maxwell warns, infiltrated by powerful multinationals. 'Quality' television may best be illustrated not by RTVE's adaptations of literary classics but by Telecinco's re-creations of North American workplace dramas. And 'television' itself is hardly self-sufficient, embedded as it is in multimedia holding companies that embrace print, music and cinema. Telecinco itself has recently funded major feature films, including Alex de la Iglesia's *Muertos de risa* (*Dying of Laughter*) (1999). I have argued, however, that these terms are not to be abandoned too soon by cultural critics dazzled by globalization and neglectful of programme content. *Periodistas* is significant as a genuine innovation in distinctively national programming in a country in which (unlike the UK or USA) there is no lasting tradition of domestic TV drama. If *Periodistas'* production values or plotting do not reach the standard of its Hollywood models, they clearly fulfil the stated aims of Telecinco's 'quality' policy documents. And *Periodistas'* enviable ratings and share demonstrate the uncanny persistence of the networks, still able to unite the nation around an 'event' programme in the supposed age of multichannel fragmentation and digitalization. As one Telecinco executive told *Television Business International*, 'We believe the business is in the content and not in the highways' (*TBI* 1997: 23).

The shift from domestic sitcom to workplace drama (from *Médico de familia* to *Periodistas*) does register, however, what Corner calls the move from an earlier 'ideology of the home' to a more recent 'individualized commodity taste' (Corner 1999: 90), facilitated by the multichannel dispersal of uses and gratifications. As we have seen, *Periodistas* implicitly addresses this shift by incorporating *Médico*'s domesticated stars as guests into its Christmas episode, even as the fragmented and conflictive households of its regular characters testify to profound social change. Likewise, *Periodistas*' self-conscious dramatization of social issues (with journalist-protagonists typically spending twenty-four hours in a wheelchair or taking to the fashion catwalk in pursuit of their 'story') attests to the viewer's desire to be both engaged by and distracted from potentially unpleasurable problems ignored by the traditional formats of Spanish television.

Corner warns that we should avoid both 'ersatz internationalism' and 'parochial foreclosure' (1999: 3). And a recent report in *Variety* suggests a contradictory situation in which 'as Spanish and American tastes drift further apart, links between the nations' business sectors are becoming tighter' (Hopewell 1999: 33). With the prices paid by Spanish networks for US sitcoms falling from $20,000 per episode in 1998 to $12,000–15,000 in 1999, Telecinco's head of acquisitions, Aldo Spagnoli, and RTVE's new director general, Pío Cabanillas (previously based with News Corp in New York), called for co-productions with Hollywood. Wrote *Variety*: 'The call for U.S. studios to Europeanize their product for Spain coincides with the entry of cosmopolitan execs into top-level positions at Madrid-based broadcasters' (40). Speaking back to the North American juggernaut that increasingly courts foreign sales, transnational executives may, ironically, protect and foster distinctively national cultural profiles through their purchasing policy as well as their original productions.

More than twenty years ago, in their classic study of the production process of a British series, Alvarado and Buscombe (1978: 7) noted that television, the source of so many hours of fiction, was critically neglected, while the much smaller sector of theatre was overrepresented in both press and academy. The same remains true *a fortiori* of Spanish television drama, which has to my knowledge received no academic attention, while analysis of Spanish cinema (of whatever quality) has greatly increased. If television studies have, in Corner's words, been too often 'the study of a perpetual present'

(121), then the curious but valuable case of Telecinco and *Periodistas* proves that it is worth arresting for a moment the ceaseless electronic flow and stopping the press for critical examination.[10]

Appendix: *Periodistas*, episode 28 (broadcast 21 December 1998), 'Dos con leche y uno solo'

Executive producer	Daniel Écija
Writers	Olga Salvador, Mauricio Romero, Alex Pina
Script co-ordinators	Pilar Nadal, Felipe Mellizo
Associate producers	Felipe Pontón, Felipe Mellizo
Directors	Daniel Écija, Jesús Rodrigo, Begoña Álvarez
Sound	Juan Carlos Ramírez
Music	Manel Santisteban
Art director	Fernando González
Photography	David Arribas

Regular cast:	
Luis	José Coronado
Laura	Amparo Larrañaga
Clara	Belén Rueda
Blas	Alex Ángulo
Mamen	María Pujalte
José Antonio	Pepón Nieto
Willy	Joel Joan
Ana	Alicia Borrachera
Ali	Esther Arroyo

Notes

1 Maxwell has not changed his position; this statement is repeated verbatim two years later, as is his claim that Spanish programming is very similar to that of the US networks (1997: 265).
2 See D'Lugo (1997) for a similar reading of Spanish cinema caught between globalization and regionalization which does, however, pay close attention to content.
3 I cite this unpaginated website by its section titles. I have translated from the Spanish all documentation from Telecinco.
4 Print advertising for the new series also playfully blurred the boundary between news and drama, presenting the characters in mock news stories.
5 For much of its lifetime *Periodistas* has competed with TVE's domestic drama *A las once en casa* or its import *ER*.
6 Statistics from the standard independent source, SOFRES.
7 This untranslatable title is explained below.

8 See chapter appendix for complete credits.
9 See Feuer et al. (1984: 37) for MTM's characteristic use of this technique in character comedy. Unlike MTM's generic hybrids, *Periodistas* ends with an unambiguous comic 'tag' as the final credits play.
10 My thanks to Álvaro Lucas at the Telecinco Press Office for kindly providing me with a full range of print and video materials, and to Ms Maddy Conway for the loan of a video tape.

References

Alvarado, Manuel and Buscombe, Edward (1978) *Hazell: The Making of a TV Series*. London: BFI.

Anon. (1994) A la búsqueda de una nueva identidad. *Cineinforme*, 648 (April), p. 18.

Bustamante, Enrique (1995) The Mass Media: A Problematic Modernization. In Helen Graham and Jo Labanyi (eds), *Spanish Cultural Studies: An Introduction*, Oxford: Oxford University Press, pp. 356–61.

Caldwell, John Thornton (1994) *Televisuality*. New Brunswick, NJ: Rutgers University Press.

Corner, John (1999) *Critical Ideas in Television Studies*. Oxford: Clarendon Press.

del Valle, David (1997) Berlusconi Faces Fraud Charges at Tele 5. *Cable & Satellite Europe*, 165 (September), p. 10.

D'Lugo, Marvin (1997) *La teta i la lluna*: The Form of Transnational Cinema in Spain. In Marsha Kinder (ed.), *Refiguring Spain: Cinema/Media/Representation*, Durham, NC, and London: Duke University Press, pp. 196–214.

Feuer, Jane, Kerr, Paul and Vahimagi, Tise (eds) (1984) *MTM: 'Quality Television'*. London: BFI.

Grabsky, Phil (1990) Telecinco Launch under Threat. *Broadcast*, 19 January, p. 6.

Green, Jennifer (1997) Telecinco Plans Expansion into the Americas. *TV World*, December, p. 8.

Heath, Stephen (1990) Representing Television. In P. Mellencamp (ed.), *Logics of Television*, Bloomington: Indiana University Press, pp. 267–302.

Hooper, John (1995) *The New Spaniards*. London: Penguin.

Hopewell, John (1999) Spanish and US TV Go Co-Prod. *Variety*, 19–25 April, pp. 33, 38, 40.

Jordan, Barry (1995) Redefining the Public Interest: Television in Spain Today. In Helen Graham and Jo Labanyi (eds), *Spanish Cultural Studies: An Introduction*, Oxford: Oxford University Press, pp. 361–9.

Maxwell, Richard (1995) *The Spectacle of Democracy: Spanish Television, Nationalism, and Political Transition*. Minneapolis: University of Minnesota Press.

—— (1997) Spatial Eruptions, Global Grids: Regionalist TV in Spain and Dialectics of Identity Politics. In Marsha Kinder (ed.), *Refiguring Spain:*

Cinema/Media/Representation, Durham, NC, and London: Duke University Press, pp. 260–83.

Mulgan, Geoff (ed.) (1990) *Questions of Quality*. London: BFI.

El País [staff reporters] (1999) La incesante polémica sobre la TV estatal. 3 July, p. 35.

Pérez Gómez, Alberto (1998) The Granting of Private TV Licences by the Spanish Government in 1989 Considered Lawful by Supreme Court. *Iris*, 4 (1) (January), p. 8.

Schrøder, Kim Christian (1992) Cultural Quality: Search for a Phantom? In Schrøder and Michael Skovmand (eds), *Media Cultures*, London: Routledge, pp. 199–219.

Scott, Alex (1996) Stakes Rise at Telecinco. *Broadcast*, 19 July, p. 13.

Telecinco (1998a) *Informe anual 1998*. Madrid: Telecinco.

—— (1998b) Dossier de prensa de la serie *Periodistas*. 12 January.

—— (1998c) Dossier de prensa de la serie *Periodistas*. 14 September.

—— (1998d) Sinopsis del capítulo . . . 28 (21-12-98). Plot synopsis accompanying specimen videocassette.

—— (1999a) Corporate website, consulted 19 July: www.telecinco.es/telecinco/10/10_frameset.html.

—— (1999b) Seguimiento/*Periodistas*/ Marzo 1999. Press file.

—— (1999c) *Periodistas* cierra su tercer temporada batiendo su propio récord de audiencia. Press release, 20 April.

Television Business International (1997) Special issue on 'Spanish TV's New Challenges' (June).

Williams, Raymond (1974a) 'Drama in a Dramatized Society'. Inaugural Lecture, University of Cambridge. Reprinted in A. O'Connor (ed.), *Raymond Williams on Television*, London: Routledge, 1989, pp. 3–13.

—— (1974b) *Television, Technology, and Cultural Form*, London: Fontana.

2 Classic Fashion? The Adolfo Domínguez Sample Book

Fashion

> Imagine (if possible) a woman dressed in an endless garment, one that is woven of everything the magazine of Fashion says, for this garment without end is proffered through a text which is itself unending . . . This endless garment has a double dimension: on the one hand, it grows deeper through the different systems which make up its utterance; on the other hand, it extends itself, like all discourse, along the chain of words.
>
> (Barthes [1967] 1983: 42)

As Barthes suggested long ago, the status of fashion as object is unstable. Infinitely extended in a material sense (divided by designer branding, seasonal change and product differentiation), it is also semantically and socially volatile (composed, in Barthes's term, of multiple, signifying 'blocs'). Moreover, if the fashion phenomenon is complex, subject to both division and transformation (extension and 'depth'), then it is also notoriously futile and trivial: the stimulus for Barthes's early exploration of the syntagm/paradigm axis, taken from a contemporary magazine, is wilfully superficial, albeit retrospectively charged with the pathos of past vestimentary practices: 'Daytime clothes in town are accented in white.'

In this second chapter I argue, however, that as the most intimate example of the interpenetration of the economic and the aesthetic, fashion is not to be minimized. Objectifying social practice in visible form, fashion also subjectifies formal properties, rendering them personal and individual. Production, distribution and consumption thus combine with form, colour and texture. The subtle hierarchy of objects displays that minute calibration of time, space and the body (by day and night, in town and country) that Bourdieu ([1980] 1992) baptised 'habitus'.[1]

A recent specialist survey of the field begins by claiming that fashion as object must be 'dissolved and reconstituted' (Craik 1994: p. xi), based as it is on volatile relations between elite couture and everyday practice and unstably defined in relation to allied concepts such as costume, uniform and dress (pp. ix, x).[2] Fashion systems (and Craik, unlike Barthes, stresses the plural) are characterized by paradox: the triviality of trends versus the supposed artistic genius of great designers (6); the existence of mass consumption at the turn of the last century before the technologies of mass production had been harnessed (7); and the reliance of elite fashion on the 'diffusion' lines of ready-to-wear and licensing (7). Marginal components of the system thus become central: fashion magazines, dominating the designers themselves, teach sometimes sceptical consumers to assume profiles, life-styles and consumerist patterns (52); and cosmetics, scents and accessories track more precisely than garments themselves the tension between individual projection and group membership (154), attempting to 'match the transformative properties of the products' to the 'ideal attributes of the consumers, according to the practical circumstances of habitus' (162). With the feminization of consumerism, however, a significant gap remains: 'fashionless men', rendered invisible by their renunciation of both the aesthetic and the social pleasures of fashion (colour and shopping), are subject to yet more subtle product differentiation than their more showy sisters (176). I argue in this chapter for a renewed attention to male fashion in the context of what is also perhaps a paradox: the 'classic' clothing which claims to transcend time even as it subtly shifts from season to season.

Such manuals of fashion studies tend to shift between a sometimes tautologous sociology (in which the habitus serves as a horizon for both collective competence and individual performance) and an inconclusive postmodernism (which expresses both horror and pleasure at a fashion system that remains socially conservative even as it embodies cultural change) (Craik 1994: 8). One respected commentator, Elizabeth Wilson, has noted the irony that those who pioneered fashion studies appeared to derive no pleasure from their chosen object. Rather, they further denigrated it, whether on economic grounds (lamenting the conspicuous consumption of the bourgeoisie), on psychological grounds (diagnosing fashion and indeed clothing as a neurotic symptom), or on sociological grounds (lamenting a status consciousness made manifest in the 'trickle down' effect from elite to street) (Ash and Wilson 1992: pp. xii–xiii). Wilson detects a 'fashion crisis' at the end of the 1980s that is both aesthetic and economic, with the waning of that decade's design culture and the rise of ecological anti-fashion poised to 'trickle up' the social pyramid (p. xv).

More important for our purpose perhaps is the continuing crisis in fashion theory. The journal of that name recently devoted a special issue to 'Methodology' (Jarvis 1998), exposing the 'great divide' between object-based dress history and cultural studies. While the former is the province of the collector and the museum, and is frequently dismissed as descriptive or antiquarian (Taylor 1998: 338), the latter is the sphere of the academy, and is attacked with equal bitterness for its theoretical 'straitjacket' (Ribeiro 1998: 320) and a visual bias that neglects tactility: 'the weight and volume' of the artefact (Ribeiro 1998: 323). Three trends are noted for this paradigm shift from object to theory: the rise of feminism and of cultural studies and the shift in academic attention from production to consumption (Styles 1998: 385). However, a more subtle institutional fissure underlies disciplinary developments: the study of dress was pioneered by women collectors in the metropolises of New York, London and Paris whose passion was 'anathema to male museum staff' (Taylor 1998: 341). The methodological divide remains, therefore, a gender divide also, with object-focused women scholars resenting the imperialism of male theorists (often trained in politics or economics) who neglect 'fashion, style, and seasonal change' (Taylor 1998: 346) and scorn the detailed empirical labour required of 'hemline histories'.

Museum curators (overwhelmingly women) are caught in this double bind, attacked for two kinds of triviality: 'musty antiquarianism and superficial glitz' (Steele 1998: 334). Arguing, however, that 'a museum of fashion is more than a clothes bag', one curator sets out a suggestive methodology for addressing artefacts as culturally expressive witnesses to material culture.[3] First comes the description of the object: a precise, formal account that remains internal to its own boundaries (Steele 1998: 329). Second comes deduction: the exploration of the sensory experience of the object by the observing (touching, wearing) subject. Finally comes speculation: the intellectual framing of questions and hypotheses tested against external evidence (Steele 1998: 331). When the museum is the locus and stimulus for such loving investigation, it is no longer 'a cemetery for dead clothes' (Steele 1998: 334). Rather, it becomes a laboratory for the revival of women's pleasure and women's labour. If the fashion object retains the fragmentary and disparate qualities of the sample books stored in museums,[4] then fashion studies can be inspired by that same plurality, breaching the divide between object and theory (aesthetics and economics) in the 'contested terrain' (Styles 1998: 383) that is 'social life made visible' (Taylor 1998: 355).

Classic fashion

The abiding complexity of fashion photography – as of fashion itself – derives from the transaction between 'the perfect' (which is, or claims to be, timeless) and 'the dated' (which inexorably discloses the pathos and absurdity of time).

(Susan Sontag, quoted in Craik 1994: 93)

John Harvey's *Men in Black* (1995), from which I take the definition of fashion as visible social life, is one of the few interdisciplinary works welcomed by fashion specialists. Concerned with the intersection of 'clothes, colour, and meaning' (9), Harvey, a literary critic by training, traces two paradoxical absences through history: the renunciation of colour and the renunciation of men. As he writes in his introduction, 'this colour – the colour that is without colour, without light, the colour of grief, of loss, of humility, of guilt, of shame – has been adopted in its use by men not as the colour of what they lack or have lost, but precisely as the signature of what they have: of standing, goods, mastery' (10). Appealing to Barthes's synchronic concern with 'that broad but especially evanescent meaning . . . of "fashionableness"' (12), Harvey also traces diachronically how 'meanings accrue, thickening over time by accretion of usage' (13).

Conspicuously self-effacing, black both represents 'social immobility' and serves to 'hide, and thus assist, surreptitious social change' (15). Black is the 'negation of the feminine', yet it can also serve, when worn by Marlene Dietrich or Madonna, as the 'negation of the gender distinction itself' (16). Stressing tactility as well as visuality ('the close value of clothes is clear . . . in the ways in which we touch our clothes' (17), Harvey asks 'whose funeral' is implicit in the perpetual mourning of the nineteenth-century bourgeoisie, whose purpose is served by the Great Masculine Renunciation that followed the French Revolution (27). The sobriety of the aristocratic dandy, dependent on simplicity, neatness and 'cut' (29), thus testifies at once and alternately to 'bourgeois chic', male narcissism (32), military discipline (34), industrial manufacturing (35) and sexual attractiveness:

the beauty of black-clad, dark figures such as Charlotte Brontë's Mr Rochester (36).

Through his minute and paradoxical pursuit of these twin absences, then, Harvey reveals (like Barthes) both the extension and the depth of the fashion system. Moreover, he charts the rise of a fashionless fashion that we may call classic, exemplified by the man's dinner jacket that has remained unchanged for 150 years. Paradoxically, therefore, apparently discreet and static male fashion reveals more subtle product differentiation than female fashion, weighted as the latter is with the burden of conspicuous display. And, making a strategic shift from consumption back to production, recent historical scholarship has argued that this proliferation of product differentiation has been integral to 'the manufacture of the fashion system'.

Historian Ellen Leopold writes that recent critical emphasis on consumer demand has neglected the 'determining role . . . played by clothing production and its history' (1992: 101). Stressing, like many commentators, the 'hybridity' of fashion (at once 'a cultural phenomenon' and 'an aspect of manufacturing'), Leopold takes turn-of-the-century New York as a test case for her interpretation of the evolution of fashion as the 'specific historical development' of clothing production.[5] Most particularly (most ironically and tragically), the 'rapidly changing proliferation of style' was a 'substitute for technical innovation' and 'the industry's failure ever fully to embrace mass production techniques' (102). While Marx had predicted that the sewing machine would do away with 'the murderous, meaningless caprices of fashion', the new technology simply 'increased the complexity of [female] dress' (105). Undercapitalized and undeveloped (107), the industry experienced 'increasing fragmentation . . . at a time when other[s] were moving rapidly towards increasing integration and concentration' (108). The continuing preference for made-to-measure over machine-made products led to an 'open-ended system of product differentiation' in which market fragmentation was used as a means of increasing the volume of sales (109). In the first half of the twentieth century a series of production changes both widened differentiation and prevented modernization: the substitution of 'little ticket' for 'big ticket' items (blouses and skirts for dresses) (110); 'price lining', whereby suppliers 'built' the quality of garments up or down for retailers (112); the introduction of new fabrics such as rayon, which allowed price reduction without technological updating (114). With constant differentiation in apparel now, for the first time, the norm at all levels of the market, 'dresses came to be marketed more like perishables' (115), in the manner of milk or citrus fruits.

Leopold ends with a paean to a 'trickle up' product, evidence for a demand for the distinct qualities of machine-made, mass-produced garments: the long-lived and 'truly popular' Levi 501 jeans. In Europe, at least, time has not proved her point: in the 1990s jeans were eclipsed by chinos, cargo and combat trousers. It remains the case, however, that the cultural studies emphasis on consumption both pathologized fickle female shoppers and neglected essential characteristics of the production and marketing process, unique to the clothing industry. A glance at the UK retail magazine *Drapers Record* (1999) confirms the continuing existence of Leopold's archaic production practices in an increasingly integrated European market. The Spanish Mango expands into Germany, Austria and France, while the Galician Zara plans seventy stores in the UK (6). Britain's 'Tesco ups Eastern European presence', while Cannes trade fair MAPIC welcomes 300 participants (including Benetton, Gap and Spanish chain Cortefiel). Mango, once more, is awarded top prize for 'retail concept and attention to detail of the shop-fits' (Zara had won in 1996 and 1998) (7). Meanwhile, the *Drapers Record* conference focused on on-line retailing (4), a development that indignant correspondents claimed would 'never replace the "touch and feel" element in buying or the retail therapy of shopping' (11). The academic debate on visuality and tactility is here replayed in a ruthlessly commercial setting.

However, globalizing abstraction is contrasted with localist archaism. 'Price-lining' lives on: suppliers are forced to accept lower prices by hard-pressed retailers (8). At an unusually high point in the economic cycle, manufacturers and store owners, both large and small, undertake 'restructuring' to improve their chances of survival (9). In uncertain times industry leaders (like Harvey's nineteenth-century bourgeoisie) turn to the understated, but apparently reliable, standards of the classic: *Drapers Record*'s lead feature is 'Brand Values: Our Essential Guide to What's Happening in the World of Classic Brands'. Surprisingly, perhaps, these 'classics' are also subject to constant structural change: German Escada plans a new offer of 'accessories that stand alone'; Dutch Bandolera launches a toiletries line in the belief that 'retail is moving towards a lifestyle offer' (p. iii); German Sandra Pabst shifts for autumn/winter 2000/1 from a 'transitional collection which bridged the gap between classic and contemporary' to 'the latest trends for a contemporary market' (p. iv). 'Classic', like black, is thus a volatile term, both praised for its timelessness and scorned for its lack of contemporaneity.

If classic production values (however defined) are increasingly international, retailing remains local. 'E-tailing', we are told, will not replace the tactile therapy of city centre shopping; and features on retail display reveal that the product differentiation lamented by Leopold is, in an increasingly standardized market, projected onto the outlets themselves. One 'doyenne of display', who waxes lyrical on 'windows [as] the eyes to the soul of the brand' (24) and as 'the art of seduction [that] tells passers-by [of] a dream that they should be buying into', also confesses that 'in the fashion industry you are working with a fairly similar product at all market levels and visual differentiation is therefore absolutely essential' (24). Or again, one mannequin supplier who stresses the limitations for retailers when 'every decision you make has to conform to the brand criteria' also claims that 'the ultimate . . . is to have a figure that completely differentiates you from the rest of the high street' (26). Designer branding, seasonal change and product differentiation thus remain the norm in contemporary European retail, as in Harvey's Victorian London and Leopold's turn-of-the-century New York. And the ostentatious austerity of the classic (dinner jacket or Levi's 501) is as volatile as ever in its semantic and social implications.

Spanish fashion

The history of costume reveals how the bourgeoisie has repeatedly replaced the aristocracy's ostentatious distinguishing marks with marks that are more restrained, more discreet, though no less formidable in terms of symbolic effectiveness.

(Beatrix Le Wita, quoted by Taylor 1998: 353)

Any visitor from the UK or the USA will be struck by Spaniards' relatively high degree of adhesion to that broad but evanescent category of 'fashionableness'. By day or night, in town or country, the Spanish style is at once more aesthetically coherent and more socially disciplined than that of looser, more diverse Anglo-American tastes. Connoisseurs of brand values, faithful to seasonal change, and devoted to product differentiation, Spanish consumers remain relatively uniform, lacking the vibrant street or anti-fashion of, say, London, even in the metropolitan centres of Madrid and Barcelona. Harvey claims that 'it was Spain, more than any other nation, that was to be responsible for the major propagation of solemn black both throughout Europe and in the New World' (Harvey 1995: 72). Black-clad monarchs such as Charles V and Philip II, who dressed with 'citizen-like modesty' (77), might be seen as precursors of the relatively severe bourgeois chic of contemporary Spaniards, whose distinctive dress relies on that cultural consensus known as the habitus. The Museum of Decorative Arts in Madrid (the nearest to a fashion museum in the capital) also features austere monochrome embroidery of the seventeenth and eighteenth centuries: stylized floral or animal motifs worked in black wool or silk (now faded to brown) on a background of natural linen or cotton, relieved only by occasional highlights in red.

Ana Martínez Barreiro (1998) of the University of A Coruña has recently published a valuable statistical analysis of the consumption of fashion in the Spanish state, based on the kind of empirical data often neglected by Anglo-Saxon advocates of the primacy of consumption. Claiming that fashion has three functions (distinction, the regulation of social change and seduction (9)), Martínez Barreiro traces a now familiar shift from Bourdieu's social hierarchization, in which a class-based cultural capital generates differentiated life-styles (13), to postmodern narcissism, which demotes collective seasonal couture and promotes individualist or tribal fragmentation (16–17). The quest for social recognition has thus, she claims, been replaced by the search for comfort, utility and solitary pleasure (17).

This international diagnosis is, however, somewhat contradicted by Martínez Barreiro's national data, based on a survey carried out all over Spain in 1994–5. Spaniards claim to follow fashion closely: 64 per cent say that they 'keep up to date' with current trends (33). But the importance attributed to forms of dress is socially hierarchized: it is not only women and the unmarried who claim competence, but informants who are educated and professional (48–9). And while men show increasing interest in fashion (almost 40 per cent believe that it is not merely 'a matter for women' (58)), the belief that fashion is of interest to the majority of the population directly correlates with educational achievement and professional status (58–9). Moreover, while subjective criteria such as 'comfort' and 'fit' are evenly distributed amongst social classes, the quest for 'quality' (as opposed to 'value') is monopolized by those who already have access to the aesthetic and social benefits of cultural capital (86–7). Interestingly, brand awareness decreases with age: it is teenagers, not managers, who assert tribal allegiance through distinctive labels.

In spite of her introduction, then, Martínez Barreiro's conclusion coincides with Bourdieu's hermetic analysis of the habitus: there is a structural homology between life-style, social class and even retail outlets. At a time of rapid change in distribution (the rise of mail order and bargain warehouses), the Spanish bourgeoisie still choose to shop in city centre designer stores and to follow the dictates of the 'season' rather than those of individual need (131). Martínez Barreiro's claim that such 'quality' consumers take part in an 'active, productive, and interpretative process' (132) is also hard to justify, given that dominant categories such as men and the married view fashion as a means to 'a correct appearance', rather than as 'a form of self-expression' (133). In spite of evidence for the 'decreasing austerity of male fashion', the 'classic suit' remains for both sexes a necessary index of 'cultural and expressive competence' and 'legitimizing taste' (135–6).

Martínez Barreiro makes no reference to specific brands or garments, and thus offers no evidence for the relative status of domestic and foreign brands in Spain. But turning from consumption to production, we see more crudely perhaps the inextricability of the aesthetic and the economic, the cultural and the industrial. The Socialist government of the 1980s placed particular emphasis on fashion, setting up in 1985 the Centre for the Promotion of Design and Fashion (Spanish CPDM) under the auspices of the Ministry of Labour and Energy. This industrial policy sought to 'manage ministerial plans relative to manufacturers' (CPDM 1991: unpaginated), just as the Ministry of Finance sought to regulate and stimulate textile and clothing production in the same year (Ministerio de Hacienda 1985). A further plan emerged in 1987 to promote 'quality, design, and fashion for the small and medium size manufacturer' (Ministerio de Industria y Energía 1987). Institutions and exhibitions proliferated: the CPDM had a library at the Ministry high up on the Castellana, as did the rival Comité de Moda (Fashion Committee) downtown by Colón. Barcelona staged a historical exposition of ready-to-wear and designer couture ('Spain: Fifty Years of Fashion') in 1988; Murcia mounted a 'homage to Spanish designers' in 1990, celebrating elite brands such as Adolfo Domínguez and Pedro del Hierro. Interestingly, these public events acknowledged the increasing creative and commercial contribution of the most isolated, underdeveloped and rural community of the state: Galicia.

The catalogue of the Murcia exhibition (Diseñadores españoles 1990), written by the director of the CPDM, makes clear the symbolic value of fashion to Socialist Spain. Acknowledging the 'close relation' between fashion and industry, consumption and production, and 'taste' and the economy, the introduction claims that the 'cultural industries' are now predominant in the 'most developed countries'. As elite fashion gives way to mass, hand-made to machine-made, and dressmaker to chain store, design must be 'incorporated into business and the new fashion culture implanted in our country'. Claimed as an 'example of political and social change with high levels of economic growth', Spain must now 'assume the challenge of incorporation into Europe', an 'opening of borders' that will 'introduce new demands in consumption'. This dissolution of frontiers is, however, 'a stimulus for [Spanish] differentiation and identity', for fashion is quite simply 'a modernizing symbol of Spanish society'.

Such initiatives may have proved more potent symbolically than commercially: Spanish fashion remains relatively undercapitalized and undeveloped. And ten years later (with the abolition of the institutional support provided by the Socialists) the evidence is contradictory. In 1999 the capital's fashion show, the Cibeles, was chaotic, 'desperately seeking an identity' when the majority of established designers had chosen not to participate (Salas 1999). The main trend for *El País* was a return to crumpled fabrics, echoing the 'heroic years' of 'the beautiful crease' once championed by Domínguez. Del Hierro was also singled out for his 'fusion of poetry and professionalism' (Salas) or 'poetry and mathematics' (Muñoz 1999), exploiting asymmetrical lines and high-tech fabrics. Spanish magazines tend to mix domestic and foreign brands in their fashion features: *El País*'s Sunday supplement story on mohair (López de Haro 1999), a textured fabric typical of trends for the autumn 1999 season, matches Spanish Sibylla (a survivor of the *movida*) with UK chain Marks & Spencer; and Galicians Domínguez and Purificación García with Italian Max Mara. *Tiempo*'s glossy supplement on 'trends for 2000' (*Tiempo* 1999) also oscillates: when local celebrities are featured, they sport subdued Spanish classics (Domínguez's textured grey knitwear is once more prominent); but erotic underwear layouts or flashy party shots rely more on the foreign glamour of Versace and Vuitton.

Tiempo also gives a 'who's who' of Spanish fashion, claiming with Galician designer Roberto Verino that the nation is now a 'genuine world power in fashion' (5). In its bullish survey of the 'most prestigious brands in the domestic territory', *Tiempo* cites both established up-market names (Del Hierro with his deal with chain Cortefiel, Domínguez with 100 own-label shops) and new challengers (Amaya, Arzuaga, who shows in London, and Purificación García, who will have sixty stores in Spain by 2000). It also calls attention to successful mid-market chains: Mango (whose European expansion caught the attention of *Drapers Record*) and Zara (founded in A Coruña and now boasting 375 stores world-wide). A symbolic focus for national pride, especially within the field of classic dress for the professional class, Spanish fashion might now appear to have achieved the international profile planned for it by the Socialists. A close corporate study of its most prominent and long-lasting label will put this hypothesis to the test.

Adolfo Domínguez: the brand

The wide range of garments and accessories by 'Adolfo Domínguez' has always had the special label of its author, identifying it with a certain life-style or mode of being that, in the final analysis, is more lasting than fashion itself.

(Adolfo Domínguez 1999c: 18)

Adolfo Domínguez, the brand, has much in common with a British competitor, Paul Smith. Both shelter behind ostentatiously unassuming names; both prefer the traditional title of 'tailor' to the more pretentious 'designer'; both are amongst a tiny number to have expanded successfully beyond an undercapitalized home territory into the EU and East Asia.[6] And if Paul Smith invented 'classics with a twist', Adolfo Domínguez, in a slogan equally celebrated in Spain, offered classics with a crease: under the banner 'the wrinkle is beautiful', Adolfo Domínguez draped the new aristocracy of the Socialist Spain of the 1980s in loose, crumpled linen. It was one of the clearest examples in history of the use of fashion both to objectify social practice in visual form and to regulate social change, and it did not go unnoticed by dandyish media commentators such as Francisco Umbral (1993: 119).

Since this self-proclaimed revolution, the aesthetic qualities of Adolfo Domínguez's brand have remained remarkably consistent, despite seasonable variation, in adherence to the timeless quality of the classic. A broad description of Adolfo Domínguez's endless garment (now disseminated and differentiated over twenty years) would stress the characteristically minimalist and rationalist forms (soft, unstructured tailoring), the severely restricted palette (black, grey, aubergine), and the richly textured fabrics (brushed and felted cotton, shaggy alpaca and mohair, distressed silk). As fashion curators recommend, Adolfo Domínguez pays as much attention to tactility as to visuality; in fact, the austerity of look for the viewer is transposed into a luxuriously intimate experience of touch for the owner, the aesthetic rendered subjective and personal once more.

Indefinitely extended, Adolfo Domínguez's brand has also acquired semantic depth, thickened by the passing of time and the accumulation of associations. Thus the tension between austerity and luxury

4 Adolfo Domínguez: Spring–Summer, 1999. Courtesy of Adolfo
Domínguez.

5 Adolfo Domínguez: Spring–Summer, 1999. Courtesy of Adolfo Domínguez.

is echoed by the pull between innovation and tradition. Adolfo Domínguez is as proud of its high-tech textiles (rubberized or with a metallic sheen) as it is of its labour-intensive natural fibres. Indeed, the brand often combines the two, exploiting contrasting textures: a fragile cobweb of silver threads overlays a shaggy woolen sheath. 'Little ticket' separates (modest long-sleeve T-shirts and trousers) are juxtaposed in shop windows with 'big ticket' avant-garde gowns, boasting asymmetrical neck- and hem-lines and exploiting a sculptural sense of volume. The typical 'simplicity' and 'practicality' of the brand are here enriched by the flashes of artistic 'genius' required of the author's signature. Bread-and-butter garments (the man's jacket remains Adolfo Domínguez's best-selling line) are subject to more subtle product differentiation: typically narrow lapels (all suits are single-breasted) sometimes disappear altogether in a homage to the Mao suit of the 1960s.

Rich and austere (richly austere), traditional in its innovations, Adolfo Domínguez also exploits the contradictory attractions of country and city. One life-style accessory is a notebook bound in natural, uncoloured straw; it is posed in a window next to a small pile of urban tools: the understated ties and brief-cases of the cultured executive. But the thrust of Adolfo Domínguez's unstructured tailoring is to unsettle the division between rural and urban, casual and formal, and indeed between male and female. The natural shoulders and crumpled fabrics, the softly draped silhouettes and subtly modulated colours, speak of a muted interzone between sharply differentiated social spaces and gendered habitus. The weight and volume of such garments invite the body to relax, even as they confer on it the formidable symbolic effectiveness of discreet distinction.

We have moved from the formal description of the observer to the sensory deduction of the wearer. Finally, we can offer a speculative hypothesis to be tested against external sources: namely, that Adolfo Domínguez's brand practises a double ascesis. Renouncing the ostentatious display and conspicuous consumption of, say, Versace and Vuitton, it also denies itself the dandyish perfection of cut that accentuates the body form in, say, Armani and Dior. The target demographic of such fashionless fashion is thus as confident of his or her social standing and of his or her personal attributes: neither need be underlined. This twin renunciation (which corresponds in part to the incorporation of Spanish women into the managerial class) delivers to both sexes the privileges of Harvey's men in black. Self-denial emphasizes not what consumers lack or have lost, but rather what they possess: the automatic authority owed to the timeless classic.

6 Adolfo Domínguez: Spring–Summer, 1999. Courtesy of Adolfo
Domínguez.

Adolfo Domínguez's own corporate sources (a website and annual report, black in one light, dull brass in another) confirm this consumer profile. Matching the product's properties to the shopper's ideal attributes, Adolfo Domínguez's marketing department tells us that its select 'upper and upper middle' audience is aged '30–45' (Adolfo Domínguez 1999c: 18), and that its newly introduced male fragrances (often the most sensitive social index) are identified with the modern, professional, cultured, and refined man. This distinct sensibility is consistently enforced by catalogues and visual merchandising (windows and mannequins) that conform to clear, but contradictory, brand criteria. Thus the catalogue for Autumn/Winter 1999 (Adolfo Domínguez: 1999b) features unstructured capes and coats in grey or natural felt and alpaca, joined only with the most archaic of fastenings: perilous hat pins or rectangular metal brooches. Yet this very Spanish-looking model (a pale-skinned brunette, hair roughly pulled back) is shot amongst the skyscrapers and subway stations of Manhattan (where Adolfo Domínguez has no store). Sitting in a shadowy stairwell, the model wears a sheer plastic raincoat over a delicately textured cotton dress. Or again, male catwalk shots feature suits teamed with T-shirts but with no tie in sight. The catalogue format thus clearly reinforces the volatile mix of rural and metropolitan, natural and artificial, and casual and formal that we deduced from analysis of the garments themselves.

The curious combination of austerity and luxury persists in Adolfo Domínguez's own label shop-fits. Just as the Adolfo Domínguez logo is unassuming (a sans serif A and D in matching black boxes), so the stores' signage is inconspicuous, barely visible from twenty yards away in a crowded street. Rational and minimal (all blond wood and glass), the interior design nevertheless allows traditionalist or modernist accentuation, grounding a global enterprise in local space. The Nancy store in France features a large, art nouveau stained glass skylight; one Madrid branch (Serrano, 18) boasts a sinuous, aluminium staircase. Product displays are consistent, yet subtly differentiated. The same mannequins recur throughout: soft, featureless dummies, impersonal adult versions of the rag doll. Yet they are posed in an infinite variety of ways. In an autumnal London they gathered sociably around a metal bench in Regent Street, but slumped dejectedly on wooden boxes in Covent Garden. Retail display thus engages a new urban geography, visible only intermittently to the consumer whose seduction it seeks and whose therapy it promotes. Serrano, 18 is directly opposite Madrid's Museum of Archeology; the windows of the showcase Paris store reflect the neoclassical pillars of the Madeleine Church opposite; spend 400 francs in the Carousel store, and lucky shoppers will be rewarded with a suitably distinctive free gift: a ticket to the adjoining Louvre Museum which frees them from the burden of queuing for entrance with common tourists. Internet marketing sites, reinforcing rather than replacing the tactile experience of city centre shopping, reveal new urban divisions unshown on printed maps: on-line shopping guide go-london tells us that Adolfo Domínguez's Regent Street store is within 'Men's Retail Area B2' (go-london 1999). The graduated retail grid is thus traced as lightly over the unsuspecting and familiar street patterns as any eruv. Conversely, a press release from the Regent Street Association, dated February 1998, basks in the distinction accorded the thoroughfare by Adolfo Domínguez's patronage: his new store is evidence for the 'retail renaissance' of a once neglected, but still classically grand, crescent. Fashion production and consumption thus form as hermetic a circle as any in Bourdieu's habitus, magically matching subjective dispositions to objective conditions.

Indeed, if we turn to production processes, then one distinguishing characteristic that Adolfo Domínguez claims for itself on its corporate website is the 'vertical integration' of brand, product and style (Adolfo Domínguez 1999d: 'Estructura vertical'). Claiming to be pioneers since 1991 of such a system (although it is clearly reminiscent of 'just in time' supply chains common to manufacturer-retailers as distinct as Marks & Spencer and Benetton), Adolfo Domínguez 'integrates design, production, promotion, and distribution'. Flexible and immediate response thus guarantees (or so we are told) a 'dynamic collection that evolves during the season': reducing risk and matching supply to real-time demand. And the corporate history of Adolfo Domínguez reveals, in spite of the brand's aesthetic appeal to the archaic and hand-made, an innovatory engagement with modern technology. In autumn 1999 the brand had twenty-five years of experience in the Spanish market, and claimed ten years at the top of domestic fashion. It boasted 135 shops in Europe, Latin America, Japan, China and South-East Asia, 700 employees and a profit of 1.3 billion pesetas on a turnover of 11.5 billion pesetas (Adolfo Domínguez 1999d: 'Perfil'). An industrial group which now has seven distinct national subsidiaries in addition to the parent company, Adolfo Domínguez's origin lies in a family tailor business whose first shop opened in its native Orense, or Ourense (Galicia), in 1973. After experience in Paris and London, Adolfo Domínguez himself launched a new line in up-market, urban ready-to-wear, opening stores in Madrid and Barcelona in 1982 and showing his first women's collection on the Paris catwalks in 1985. Expansion in

Europe and Asia followed, with diffusion into a moderately priced line, 'Básico', and licensed perfume (1986 and 1991, respectively). After management restructuring made possible by advanced computer links through the chain, Adolfo Domínguez went public on the Madrid Stock Exchange in 1997 (Adolfo Domínguez 1999d: 'Orígenes'), a launch so successful that the shares doubled in price in the first day's trading.

The distinctiveness of this corporate history is corroborated by the financial press and by the general media. Adolfo Domínguez, the brand and the person, consistently bounces back after misfortune: a disastrous fire in 1991 proved a spur to renewed modernization (Anon. 1991). And the continuing media narrative subjectivizes the label, blurring the distinction between commercial and personal profiles. An ascetic aesthete, Adolfo Domínguez's much publicized life-style is the very image of the dandy's self-discipline. Industrious, austere, frugal and sober, Domínguez's personal authority is based on his renunciation of facile pleasures, even those of fashion: he has repeatedly claimed to be more interested in other, more prestigious arts, and has indeed authored a novel and produced a feature film. But one aspect of the brand only implicit in its products and retail strategy is explicit in interviews: the Galician localism of this global company. Thus *El País* presents him as a 'mystic tailor' (Verdú 1997); *El Periódico* as a 'strange ascetic' (Iborra 1997); *El Exportador* as a 'global Galician' (Lázaro 1997); and *Actualidad Económica* as a 'brave little tailor' from a 'magical land' (Cambra 1998). 'Entrepreneur of the year' in *Cinco Días* (Anon. 1998), the diminutive, simply dressed figure (always in black jacket and polo neck) is still patronized by the metropolitan media for his rural background and stubborn loyalty to the Ourense, which remains his manufacturing and administrative headquarters. Exemplary of the opening of borders and the incorporation of Spain into the world, promoted by the Socialist government with which Adolfo Domínguez was so closely identified, still the brand remains volatile, its cultural capital vulnerable to the aesthetic and economic contradictions that inform it.

Adolfo Domínguez: The Season

[Adolfo Domínguez's] modern, elegant, plain, and very practical style combines northern sobriety and southern warmth in the simple, unstructured forms that have become, since the beginning of Adolfo Domínguez's career, the unmistakable seal of his brand.

(Adolfo Domínguez 1999c: 19)

The central problem of fashion and fashion studies is the conflict between continuity and discontinuity. How can the timeless values of the classic brand be reconciled with the constant demand for product differentiation and seasonal change? Surely the endless quest for innovation betrays at once the futility and triviality of the fashion system and (in Sontag's words) the pathos and absurdity of time? Postmodern commentators, in Spain and elsewhere, have proclaimed the end of the season: solipsistic consumers at street level, we are told, now pay little attention to collective dictates handed down by the elite. But production is, as we have seen, linked ever more closely to consumption with the vertical integration of the 'just-in-time' supply chain. And the erosion of retail boundaries (in which a little tailor from Galicia comes to own stores from Tokyo to Buenos Aires) is dependent on a sensitivity of response to demand which inscribes the local into the global. As we shall see, the season is not dead, but rather divided: targeted to distinct territories and market segments, modulated by customer preference in real time. It is a process with many 'authors': designers, journalists (both specialist and general), window dressers and customers.

In August 1999 American *Vogue* predicted 'Red Rules' for Fall (200). The cover feature, shot against a wintry New York full of black-clad security guards and paparazzi, showed lipstick-red coats with tailored waists, cherry Vuitton luggage, carmine crushed silk boots, and Rouge Sensation cosmetics from Lancome. Yet other stories in the same issue contradict this very clear message. 'Metropolitan' tells us that nothing says 'urban' more than 'laser-sharp tailoring . . . and plenty of New York black' (178); 'Ruche hour' (194) features 'delicate gathering [to] add feminine texture' to accessories in black, white and bourdeaux; and 'Suit yourself' (252) showcases 'cooler, softer alternatives' to the business suit, all in the shade of cream, which, we are told, 'rises to the top'. By November, mid-market trends in Britain were for animal prints (echoing *Vogue*'s recent promotion of fur), tweed flares and long A-line skirts; the 'Style Police' claimed that 'last winter's grey gives us a . . . mild depression', and recommends Zara's 'natural fabrics with techno touches' and a 'clash colour palette' of orange, turquoise and cerise (Sherwood 1999). Finally, *Drapers Record* reported on the actual best-selling colours on the UK high street for October: black, grey, olive-green and burgundy.

The autumn season was thus, in the words of Style Police, 'all over the place', with green taking over from red as the hottest high-fashion shade. Related to this was the millennial mixture of natural and techno praised in Zara: *Tiempo*'s style supplement likewise combined a pouf made of natural straw with sleek shiny gadgets such as a tiny videophone. Adolfo Domínguez coincided with what Andrew Ross has called 'cyborg green' (1994: 230). Contemporary interviews in *El Mundo* and *Ronda Iberia* had seen him claim ('clinging like a raccoon to the tree bark, submerged like a dolphin in the water') that 'the debate between Adam Smith and ecology is false' and that 'we must ruralize the cities' (Pita 1998); or agreeing that the natural greys and browns of Galicia remain an influence on this 'multinational impresario' even as he harnesses computers to his production process (Quintero 1998). Adolfo Domínguez's palette for 1998 had also relied on natural notes: 'dark and sober tones with luminous touches of ochre, aubergine, and mauve for women; the widest range of greys, forest green, midnight blue, and dark cherry for men' (1999c: 18–19).

The two catalogues for the 1999 seasons stayed on message. Copy in Spring/Summer (1999a) promised a 'luxurious ecology': 'Just as a beautiful face is not harmed by wrinkles, so a beautiful fabric is yet more so when it does not hide its imperfections.' Elsewhere, 'formal and casual [lines] fuse in simple forms'; fabrics are superimposed, shot through with metal thread, or permanently wrinkled by twisting; full-length dresses in white and black feature frayed asymmetrical hem-lines: 'subtly unfinished finishes'. The life-style offer of such imperfect perfection is made explicit at the end of the catalogue: drawings with swatches of identical grey fabric promote Adolfo Domínguez's 'Essential Quintet': matching jackets, skirts and trousers for all the working woman's needs. The Autumn/Winter catalogue (1999b) stresses fabric over colour, touch over eye: alpaca, used only in its natural shades, has 'unique thermal properties' derived from its Andean origin; silk, unprofitable in its production, 'may die out at any moment . . . now beauty is no longer prized in human life'. The global designer thus takes under his elegant wing the world's most threatened creatures and fabrics, in a gesture of ecological anti-fashion that serves only to reconfirm the classical distinction of his seasonal line.

On European high streets it was not red but grey that ruled. Fashionable consumers draped themselves in charcoal flares and chunky mixed knits, Adolfo Domínguez's sober stock-in-trade, from Madrid to London. But by December Regent Street was split in two: Benetton's flagship boasted all grey in one window and the clashing citrus palette recommended by Style Police in the other. Turning on a dime, the season responded 'just in time' to consumers apparently depressed by the grey already twelve months out of date in high fashion. Adolfo Domínguez's Madeleine store in Paris also broke ranks: facing one way with full-price Galician greys and browns, the other with disconcertingly strident lime and orange in the Básico range. Northern sobriety and southern warmth were thus juxtaposed in an unstable, even inconsistent, manner that surely failed to reinforce the all-important brand criteria.

One garment featured in windows in all three cities that autumn was an unassuming long-sleeved grey T-shirt (reference number 5.73.02.12222). By following the threefold methodology recommended in *Fashion Theory*, we may pay due respect to the individual object, so often neglected or devalued in academic dress study. First comes formal description. The garment has a repeated pattern of horizontal stripes of irregular width in contrasting shades of charcoal and light grey. The pattern is symmetrically matched back and front, and when the arms hang down, their pattern also coincides with that on the front panel. It has a shallow V-neck, with ribbing in light grey, and small vents at the bottom of each side. The simple AD logo is heat-impressed on the left breast, but not picked out in contrasting fabric or stitching. The cut is rectangular: loose but not baggy, hanging straight down from the shoulders and chest to just above the crotch. It thus neither emphasizes nor diminishes the body form. Inside the garment, the front of the label picks out the brand name in white stitching on dove grey; the back is lined with another tiny piece of white material. The washing instructions, at the left waist, give addresses in Spanish for licensed importers in Mexico and Argentina on the front, and claim in English that the garment is 'made in CEE [i.e. Comunidad Económica Europea]'. On the back the consumer is told that the garment is 100 per cent cotton and is to be washed by hand in cold water.

Moving from description to deduction and from vision to touch, I note that the lighter-coloured stripes are made of softer, brushed cotton, slightly raised against the smoother charcoal bands. The inside seams are raised and double machine stitched. When worn, the garment permits complete freedom of movement: it is easy to forget one is wearing it. Comparing it with other objects, I note that Adolfo Domínguez sells similar long-sleeved T-shirts in which muted burgundy or orange stripes alternate with the light grey brushed cotton. But these have crew necks and regular stripes, a less complex pattern than that of my chosen garment. A long-sleeved, V-neck T-shirt bought in the same season in chain store Marks & Spencer looks very similar to mine: unstriped, it is made of the same light grey brushed cotton. But closer inspection reveals variant details: the label is not backed, thus exposing the ugly reverse of the logo; there are no side vents; and machine washing is permitted.

The seams are less substantial and have only one line of stitching. Finally, although the size is the same, the cut is tighter: it feels both less substantial in weight and less ample in volume.

My hypothesis is that these details, invisible to the spectator, but perceptible to the wearer, embody the hierarchical distinction between designer classic and mass market chain store. Leading out from the object itself to external evidence, we can speculate (in *Fashion Theory*'s third stage) on the intellectual context in which the garment is worn and 'read'. While the feel is comfortable and practical (virtues central to Adolfo Domínguez's brand identity), the washing instructions are not, requiring as they do a return to pre-modern manual labour unwelcome to most contemporary consumers. Adolfo Domínguez's select demographic must thus suffer for their distinction, or employ hired help. Interestingly, the difference in garment care is greater than that in price: the Adolfo Domínguez garment, objectively better made and subjectively more pleasurable to wear, retails in London at just five pounds more than its Marks & Spencer's clone.[7]

Why the V-neck in the grey garment and not in the coloured? My hypothesis, once more, is that this item pushes against the unstable boundary between formal and casual wear, in a manner that corresponds to Adolfo Domínguez's published brand criteria. The long-sleeved T-shirt is in itself a novel garment of the 1990s, ambiguously placed between its more familiar cousins the shirt and the short-sleeved T-shirt, which are clearly coded as formal and informal wear, respectively. The ostentatious sobriety of our chosen example renders it fitting for some modern men to wear to work, teamed, perhaps, with one of Adolfo Domínguez's unstructured suits. Spanish males, still lacking the skills to shop on their own (Martínez Barreiro 1998: 88), can none the less employ Adolfo Domínguez's ascetic aestheticism in symbolically effective form to suggest a restraint and discretion that are softened (feminized) for the 1990s. Conjugating the classic and the contemporary, they lay claim with mute authority to the privileges of both tradition and modernity. No longer men in black, self-serving in their all too showy renunciation, but men in softer grey, they reap the rewards of a cultural competence that dares to relax only to reaffirm its narcissistic mystery.

But what of the 'made in CEE' label? Adolfo Domínguez, who makes much of his care for his work force and loyalty to manufacturers in Galicia and its historic neighbour of northern Portugal, here slips up in precisely one of those symbolic details on which, I have argued, the classic brand bases its claim to distinction. For although Adolfo Domínguez distances himself from Third World exploitation (Marks & Spencer's garment comes from Sri Lanka), his garment reveals in the mistranslated, anachronistic acronym (the Spanish for 'European Economic Community') a jarring inattention to detail. For if the global Galician, fluent in English and French, and dedicated to the dissolution of frontiers, does not know that 'CEE' should read 'EU', then surely something is amiss?

Raw hems

Madrid, September 1999: the first damp days of autumn. On Serrano's fashion strip (opposite the Archeological Museum, at the back of the National Library) the windows of Adolfo Domínguez's up-market rivals Purificación García and Pedro del Hierro show grey textured fabrics such as mohair relieved only by scarlet accessories: daytime clothes in town are accented in red. Bowing only minimally to this chromatic consensus, Adolfo Domínguez shows a rubberized mulberry raincoat and a metallic blue dress. The men's line is downstairs; women must ascend the elegant staircase. Solo male shoppers thumb discreetly through the grey racks, while a husband stands in front of the full-length mirror as his wife discusses his options. Shop assistants draped in loose-fitting natural fabrics (at once formal and casual) busy themselves and do not harass the clients. I remember that the website tells us that Adolfo Domínguez has recently employed a specialist firm to draft 'behaviour books' for its salespeople: 'raising the level of attention to our clients and objectively following income in order to link it to diverse incentive formulas' (1999d: 'Equipo humano'). When I approach an assistant, he registers not a flicker of disquiet at my less than impeccable appearance. As he attempts to remove the long-sleeved grey T-shirt I request from the rag doll mannequin, the latter falls floppily against its neighbours and must finally be propped up against the wall. A female assistant wraps the garment in tissue paper, discreetly monogrammed in tiny gold lettering, and places it in the bag: apparently black with the understated logo in white, it gleams burgundy in the autumnal light outside. I am strangely gratified by this unaccustomed experience of retail therapy and, emboldened by my bag, have no trouble hailing a taxi outside.

At this time, however, Adolfo Domínguez, the brand, was not without its problems. The 'new toy' which had exceeded all expectations when launched on the stock market in March 1997 (Anon. 1997), was now in some trouble. Official figures from the Madrid Exchange show that the share price fell from 26.59 to 13.83 euros by June 1999 (Bolsa de Madrid 1999). While the staff and turnover continued to rise year on year, profits before and after taxes have fallen steeply: by more than 30 per cent from 1998 to 1999. In his letter to shareholders (1999c: 6–8), Adolfo Domínguez admitted that his policy of rapid expansion and diversification would now have to be slowed, even as he repeated his ambition to make the label a global brand. The market was now yet more competitive at both ends: FashionClick reported in September 1998 that 'veteran Galician designer Purificación García [had] opened a vast 3-storey space' also on Serrano, with another twenty stores to open in Spain in September. At the lower mid-market, 'Galician apparel giant Inditex, owner/parent company of trendy Spanish retailer Zara', which already had its own stores in New York and London, had inked a deal for distribution throughout Germany. If Spain was now truly a force in the retail world (Inditex has a massive annual turnover of $1.4 billion), then it would seem to be at Adolfo Domínguez's expense.

When Adolfo Domínguez had taken his brand public, he had stressed the discipline of the market, which would be in the long-term interests of what had been a family business (Lázaro 1997). FashionClick (1998) reported that, ironically, it was members of Adolfo Domínguez's own family who, through their textile business, were now manufacturing and distributing Purificación García's new product line. The tension between public image and private pleasure implicit in the consumption of fashion thus here rebounded in a corporate conflict around production, pitting the collective against the individual. Adolfo Domínguez has said that, in spite of his reticence, he does not mind people thinking that behind Adolfo Domínguez (the brand) is Adolfo Domínguez (the man) (Quintero 1998). The volatility of relations between high fashion and everyday life could hardly have been better expressed than in his own corporate history.

Fashion is desire: the shifting and unstable space that opens up between ideal demand and material need, between the fantasy of perfection and the necessity for protection. If the Spanish garment industry lacks the strong identity of French or Italian equivalents, then, like German imageless fashion, it has still become a significant force in the integrated European market in which Adolfo Domínguez remains a prestigious player. Adolfo Domínguez's 'raw hems' or 'unfinished finishes', however, suggest not only the bourgeois propensity, much cited by Bourdieu, to render even the transparently unaesthetic distinctively handsome (Bourdieu [1979] 1984: 35); they also point to the loose threads in Barthes's endless garment. For if the gap between the economic and the aesthetic is not to be closed, fashion still serves as the most visible and intimate reminder of their inextricability.[8]

Notes

1 For an account of the habitus in Bourdieu, see Smith 2000: 136.
2 For an excellent collective volume on dress (and its relation to fashion), see Ash and Wilson 1992.
3 Steele's methodology is based on that of dress historian Jules Prown.
4 See Musée de la Mode 1997: 18–23 for examples of sample books (known in France as 'albums') preserved in Paris.
5 For sweatshops in contemporary New York, see Ross 1997.
6 For a recent interview with Paul Smith addressed to an Asian audience, see *Londonzok* (1999–2000): 7–9.
7 Adolfo Domínguez's T-shirt costs 4,850 pts in Madrid's Serrano and £25 in London's Regent Street, around 30 per cent more at current exchange rates.
8 My thanks to Adolfo Domínguez, SA, for kindly providing me with annual reports, catalogues and a wide range of press clippings.

References

Adolfo Domínguez (1999a) Primavera-Verano 1999 [catalogue]. Orense.
—— (1999b) Otoño/Invierno 1999 [catalogue]. Orense.
—— (1999c) *Informe anual 1998* [report]. Orense.
—— (1999d) www.adolfodominguez.es [corporate website]. Consulted 7 September.
Anon. (1991) Perfil del diseñador Adolfo Domínguez, que resurge después del devastador incendio que destruyó su taller en junio. *El País*, 24 September.
Anon. (1997) Un juguete nuevo [stock exchange report]. *El País*, 23 March.
Anon. (1998) Emprendedor del año: Adolfo Domínguez. *Cinco Días*, 21 April.
Ash, Juliet and Wilson, Elizabeth (eds) (1992) *Chic Thrills: A Fashion Reader*. London: Pandora.
Barthes, Roland ([1967] 1983) *The Fashion System*. New York: Hill & Wang.
Bolsa de Madrid (1999) Adolfo Domínguez, S.A.: consolidated data. www.bolsamadrid.es/mse/empresas/06000A01.HTM. Consulted 9 September.
Bourdieu, Pierre ([1979] 1984) *Distinction: A Social Critique of the Judgement of Taste*. New York and London: Routledge.
—— ([1980] 1992) Structures, Habitus, Practices. In *The Logic of Practice*, Cambridge: Polity, pp. 52–65.
Cambra, Pilar (1998) Adolfo Domínguez: el sastrecillo valiente [interview]. *Actualidad Económica*, June.
Centro de Promoción de Diseño y Moda (1991) *Bibliografía de diseño y moda*. Madrid: Ministerio de Industria y Energía.

Craik, Jennifer (1994) *The Face of Fashion: Cultural Studies in Fashion.* London and New York: Routledge.

Diseñadores españoles: homenaje a la moda de España (1990) Murcia: Institución Ferial.

Drapers Record (1999) 27 November.

FashionClick (1998) Barbara Barker's Fashion Short Takes. www.fashionclick.com/FashionClick4/ShortTakes6.htm. Consulted 9 September.

go-london (1999) www.go-london.co.uk/mensretail/B2listing.html. Consulted 9 September.

Harvey, John (1995) *Men in Black.* London: Reaktion.

Iborra, Juan Ramón (1997) Adolfo Domínguez [interview]. *El Periódico*, 30 March.

Jarvis, Anthea (ed.) (1998) *Fashion Theory*, 4 (December), Special Issue on Methodology.

Lázaro, María (1997) Costurero global [interview]. *El Exportador*, December.

Leopold, Ellen (1992) The Manufacture of the Fashion System. In Ash and Wilson 1992: 101–17.

López de Haro, Renée (1999) El embrujo del mohair. *El País Semanal*, 24 October.

Londonzok (1999–2000) no. 18 (December–January).

Martínez Barreiro, Ana (1998) *Hacia una nueva cultura de la moda.* La Coruña: Univerdidade da Coruña.

Ministerio de Hacienda (1985) Textiles y confecciones. In *Informe de Comercio Exterior*, Madrid, pp. 344–64.

Ministerio de Industria y Energía (1987) *Plan de promoción de calidad, diseño, y moda para la pequeña y mediana industria manufacturera.* Madrid.

Muñoz, Ana (1999) Pedro del Hierro: poesía matemática, *ABC*, 10 September.

Musée de la Mode et du Textile (1997) Special issue of *Connaissance des Arts.*

Pita, Elena (1998) Adolfo Domínguez: 'El capitalismo ha goleado al socialismo' [interview]. *El Mundo*, 19 August.

Quintero, Manuel (1998) Primer plano: Adolfo Domínguez [interview]. *Ronda Iberia*, October.

Regent Street Association (1998) Electronic press release (February); www.regent-street.co.uk/N-RENS.HTM. Consulted 9 September.

Ribeiro, Aileen (1998) Re-Fashioning Art: Some Visual Approaches to the Study of History of Dress. In Jarvis 1998: 315–26.

Ross, Andrew (1994) *The Chicago Gangster Theory of Life: Nature's Debt to Society.* London and New York: Verso.

—— (1997) *No Sweat: Fashion, Free Trade, and the Rights of Garment Workers.* London and New York: Verso.

Salas, Roger (1999) Pedro del Hierro salva la unión de poesía y oficio en la Pasarela Cibeles. *El País*, 10 September.

Sherwood, James (1999) Style Police [high street seasonal round-up]. *Independent on Sunday* (London), 7 November.

Smith, Paul Julian (2000) *The Moderns: Time, Space, and Subjectivity in Contemporary Spanish Culture*. Oxford: Oxford University Press.

Steele, Valerie (1998) A Museum of Fashion Is More Than a Clothes-Bag. In Jarvis 1998: 327–36.

Styles, John (1998) Dress in History: Reflections on a Contested Terrain. In Jarvis 1998: 381–90.

Taylor, Lou (1998) Doing the Laundry? A Reassessment of Object-Based Dress History. In Jarvis 1998: 337–58.

Tiempo (1999) Especial Tendencias 2000. November.

Umbral, Francisco (1993) *La década roja*. Barcelona: Planeta.

Verdú, Vicente (1997) Adolfo Domínguez: el sastre místico. *El País*, 9 March.

Vogue (1999) American edition, August.

3 Pure Painting?
The Miquel Barceló
Sketch Book

The rules of art

These fields are the site of the antagonistic coexistence of two modes of production and circulation obeying inverse logics. At one pole, there is the anti-'economic' economy of pure art. Founded on the obligatory recognition of the values of disinterestedness and on the denegation of the 'economy' . . . and of 'economic' profit (in the short term), it privileges production and its specific necessities, the outcome of an autonomous history . . . oriented to the accumulation of symbolic capital . . . At the other pole, there is the 'economic' logic of the literary and artistic industries which, since they make the trade in cultural goods just another trade, confer priority on distribution, on immediate and temporary success . . . and are content to adjust themselves to the pre-existing demand of a clientele.

(Bourdieu [1992] 1996: 143)

Pierre Bourdieu's *The Rules of Art* is perhaps the most ambitious of recent attempts to trace the imbrication of the aesthetic and the economic, of art and commerce. Rejecting the experience of the work of art as one of love ('an astonished abandon to the work grasped in its inexpressible singularity' (p. xv)), Bourdieu defends sociology against the charge of reductionism made by idealist philosophy. Beginning with an analysis of Flaubert's *Education sentimentale* as a test case for the paradoxical emergence of 'industrial art' in nineteenth-century Paris, Bourdieu goes on to examine in minute detail the 'historical genesis of the pure aesthetic' which proclaimed the autonomy of the artist even as it masked and enacted his or her inextricability from social, economic and political institutions. As we shall see, however, the revelation of this 'end game' ('the increasingly greater interpenetration between the world of art and the world of money' (344)) need not lead to disenchantment. Rather, for Bourdieu, it provokes ever-renewed defence of the autonomy of the intellectual.

The 'heroic phase' of this conquest of autonomy was based in the early nineteenth century on an 'ethical rupture' with the triumphalist bourgeoisie (60–1). Yet it was also founded on a paradoxical 'double negation' typified by Flaubert's rejection of both Romanticism and realism (71). If an artistic position was to be made, then, it was contradictory: the 'collective invention of . . . the heroic figure of the struggling artist' (133) is typified, after Manet, by the 'institutionalization of anomie, after which no one can claim to be absolute master and possessor of the *nomos*, of the principle of vision and legitimate division' (132). Likewise, the intellectual is defined (after Zola) by the intervention in the political field 'in the name of autonomy' (129), but only at the cost of the loss of temporal power (130). Just as the painter struggles to break free of commissions ('even the most neutral and eclectic, that of state sponsorship' (139)), so the 'autonomous' intellectual proposes that 'the artist is only responsible to himself'. Both claim to engage in 'a cultural production free of any external instruction and injunction'. However, in this 'inverted economy' (216), the artistic field becomes a game of 'loser takes all': 'it excludes the quest for profit and guarantees no correspondence of any kind between monetary investments and revenues', between the 'external hierarchization' of social success and the 'internal hierarchization' of specific peer consecration (217).

Institutional autonomy, moreover, is linked to aesthetic purity: 'The invention of the pure gaze is brought about in the very movement of the field towards autonomy . . . the assertion of the autonomy of the principles of production and evaluation of the work of art is inseparable from the assertion of the autonomy of the producer [and of] painting as a play with form, values, and colours independently of any reference to transcendent meanings' (299). It is a 'process of purification' played out by the successive revolutions of the avant-garde against artistic orthodoxy. But the 'purity' of the artist (founded on his supposed rupture with the bourgeoisie) is also based on his 'singular art of living' (58), whereby he constitutes his own (restricted) market. The modern writer or artist is thus an 'unprecedented social personage . . . a full-time professional, dedicated to [his] work in a total and exclusive manner, indifferent to the exigencies of politics and to the injunctions of morality, and not recognizing any jurisdiction other than the norms specific to [his] art' (76–7).

This symbolic revolution (after Flaubert) appears to 'make the market disappear' (81), but remains caught in the dual economic logics of pure art (long-term symbolic capital and production) and industry (short-term cultural commerce and distribution) (142–3). The nineteenth-century heroic innovation of, say, Manet is thus not so far from the twentieth-century charismatic conceptualism of, say, Duchamp, an extreme case of artistic 'purity' and autonomy reliant on an 'essentially symbolic transformation, that is performed by the attaching of a painter's signature or a couturier's label' (171). The rules of art thus include two mutually constituting examples of the *illusio*, or 'game', whereby artists and public collude: the 'production of belief' (166) in the work of art (however commercialized) and the 'institution of freedom' (257) in the artist's career (however compromised).

The ends of art

Art history, criticism, the market, and the museum mutually circulate their meanings . . . All meanings here contribute to, and are swallowed up in, the roar of *fashion* . . . a dizzy whirl whose very velocity, like a gyrating toy, guarantees its stability . . . The discourses of fashion and art journalism have flowed into an easy confluence of tone.

(Burgin 1986: 174–5)

Much Anglo-American writing on contemporary art, whether based on the philosophy of aesthetics or on more recent critical theory, takes it for granted that Bourdieu's twin modes, or poles, of art and commerce are now indistinguishable. Since the vertiginous rise of the New York art market in the 1980s, which coincided with the promotion of fashionable figures such as American neo-conceptualists Julian Schnabel and Jeff Koons or European neo-expressionists Georg Baselitz and Francesco Clemente, the aesthetic and the economic have fused, and the two worlds of art and money have merged into one. It is an intuition that even the more sober, historicizing Bourdieu confirms in his comparison of the transformative powers of the painter's signature and the couturier's label.

For veteran philosopher Arthur C. Danto, contemporary art marks 'the passing of the pure', now reduced to the 'haunting memory . . . of modernism . . . as an artistic ideal' (1997: p. xiii). Danto's opening example is the uncanny insertion by one recent artist of his own painting within a frame from Hitchcock's revered *Vertigo*. In this 'post-historical moment' the master narratives of art history have come to an end, and the Hegelian 'pale of history' (the barrier separating true art from false) no longer holds. In the narrative of high modernism constructed by Clement Greenberg (champion of the Abstract Expressionists), painting was both produced and evaluated according to a principle of purity: after Manet, 'Modernist pictures frank[ly] declared the flat surfaces on which they were painted' (7); and the cumulative history of art was that of increasingly rigorous self-examination (68). In Bourdieu's terms, the pure gaze of the evaluative critic was mirrored in the pure aesthetic of the productive artist, devoted to form, value and colour, irrespective of representation and transcendence.

Danto's post-history is rather different, finding its origin in Warhol, a figure barely mentioned by Bourdieu. The moral of the Brillo Box is that 'nothing need mark the difference' between the object in the gallery and the one in the supermarket (13). With the barrier broken between the aesthetic and the everyday, artists are now, writes Danto, 'liberated from the burden of history . . . free to make art in whatever way they wished' (15). Inverting the 'inverted economy' of heroic nineteenth-century rebellion, contemporary artists thus equate art and industry, production and distribution.

If philosopher Danto argued in the mid-1990s for 'the end of art history', psychoanalytic critic Victor Burgin treated 'the end of art theory' some ten years earlier. Burgin (whose own rigorously conceptual art practice also includes a subtle intervention in *Vertigo*) prefigures the postmodern formulae of Danto, but with a rather different edge. Burgin argues that the supposed crisis in art is actually a 'crisis in criticism' (140), steeped as it is in a 'hypnosis' or willed amnesia to its own history. Continental theory remains a 'challenge to the empirical-intuitive Anglo-Saxon critical tradition' (153), but the market has 'emptied [art] of signification [so it] become[s] a token in a universalized system of values in which money is the sole signified' (171). In recent catalogues, 'art and artists' have been unapologetically displaced by 'collections and collectors' (172), and the 'dominant form of art history in the modern period is . . . a history of, and for, the sale room' (173). For Burgin, too, fashion and art have fused: he cites samples of journalistic writing in the two fields which read indistinguishably (175). In this Lyotardian 'crisis of legitimation' (176), Burgin cites Bourdieu: 'Who is to be the producer of the value of the work: the painter or the dealer?' (189).

Finally, however, Burgin remains optimistic, claiming that 'the end of art theory' is in fact ' "the end of art" theory' (197); and that 'the end of "grand narratives" does not mean the end of either morality or memory' (198). 'Critical forms of sociality and subjectivity' thus remain possible (204). Theoretically sophisticated (positioning his critique as a Derridean 'supplement' to an art world of simulacra), Burgin remains frozen, however, in the traditional heroic pose of the struggling artist, implicitly claiming an ethical rupture with commercialism even as his 'outsiderism' (187) remains internal to the rules of the academies and galleries on which he is dependent for sponsorship and commissions. Like the nineteenth-century artist-intellectual, his ability to intervene in temporal questions is bought only at the cost of lost aesthetic purity.

Unsurprisingly, perhaps, the major US art magazines have little difficulty conjugating art and commerce in varying degrees. Thus *Art in America* can tell its readers, apparently without irony, that 'the twentieth century ended on a high note': 'While the fall art season was marked by the [New York] mayor's aggressive attack on some controversial contemporary art works, buyers for such items were out in force, as evidenced by record-breaking sales results at both houses' (Anon. 2000: 27). We are told that at Christie's Jeff Koons's ceramic sculpture *Pink Panther* provoked a 'telephone bidding war' that 'stunned the audience', selling for $1.8 million, an auction record for the artist. Meanwhile, at Sotheby's, Rothko's *No. 15* (described as a 'large red and yellow painting') fetched $11 million, 'double the high estimate'. Cheerfully transgressing the 'pale of history', the market thus embraced with equal enthusiasm postmodern irony and high-modernist purity.

The same issue of *Art in America* contained detailed reports on Mayor Giuliani's attack on the Brooklyn Museum's hosting of 'Sensation', a show of young British artists. The reports trace the complex interpenetration of private sponsorship (the exhibition was supported by British collector Maurice Saatchi, auction house Christie's, and veteran pop star David Bowie), local and national politics, and media coverage (Dubin 2000; Rosenbaum 2000). The editor of *Artnews*, meanwhile, wrote an impeccably historicist 'open letter to Mayor Giuliani', citing scandalized verdicts on earlier avant-garde transgressions ('Degas is repulsive'), including those printed by *Artnews* itself (Esterow 1999). The specialist magazines thus produce month by month a continuing commentary on the interpenetration of art, commerce and even urbanism ('Pittsburgh Cultural District Takes Shape' (Ebony 2000)), which in its minute materialism is closer to the concerns of Bourdieu than the sometimes apocalyptic essays of art philosophers and theorists. Moreover, leaping the pale once more, they combine this economic chronicle of distribution with a purely aesthetic evaluation of production: the opening sale-room narratives (run by *Art in America* in a section called 'Front Page') give way to features and reviews world-wide which are una-shamedly aesthetic in their criteria. Making the market disappear for a moment, *Artforum* dismisses Francesco Clemente's encyclopaedic retrospective at the Bilbao Guggenheim as a 'klutzy smear' (Hickey 2000). If the 'battle of Brooklyn' shows that the artist's institution of freedom can still provoke bourgeois outrage, then the attack on Clemente reveals that monetary and institutional capital are not always sufficient to produce belief in a work of art.

Contemporary Spanish art

Passages: in time, 'sanctuaries of the ephemeral'; in space, 'corridors of light'. In both dimensions, that which eludes the centre and its extension: domains of the other, of the no-place, of what is different. Time out of time or space out of space, the passage as an imaginary postulate beyond the last frontier, as extraterritorial territory. But also, in the mean-while, an unappealable displacement has led our entire culture astray, away from any centre it may have had, irrevocable habitats – none the less uncomfortable for it, less difficult to domesticate, to convert into real 'houses of men' – of any contemporary experience.

(Brea 1992: 17)

While Anglo-American commentators were proclaiming the end of art, Spanish art was experiencing a radically new beginning. The election of the Socialists in 1982 marked the end of the transition to democracy and coincided with the emergence of large numbers of artists who, for the first time, benefited from both state sponsorship and access to the outside world. From the lush figurative painters of the 1980s, such as Guillermo Pérez Villalta and Miquel Barceló, to the austere constructivist sculptors of the 1990s, such as Susana Solano and Cristina Iglesias, Spanish artists, both male and, increas-ingly, female, became part of a global art market with unprecedented national and international impact.

One commercial factor in this renaissance was the institution in 1982 of ARCO, the successful Madrid commercial art fair; and private foundations such as the Caixa (Savings Bank) of Barcelona and the Juan March in Madrid and La Palma also made substantial investments in contemporary Spanish artists. But, unlike in the USA (where commercial galleries such as those of veteran Leo Castelli or newcomer Mary Boone fed the boom), in Spain most sponsorship was public (whether from the nation-state or the new autonomous governments). Such state funding was inseparable from urban renewal: high-profile contemporary art museums, hitherto absent in Spain, were adapted from historical buildings (Madrid's Centro de Arte Reina Sofía, 1986), parachuted into decayed neighbourhoods (Barcelona's MACBA, 1995), or combined ancient and modern sites (Valencia's' IVAM, 1986). Such developments proclaimed a break with the Francoist past, most particularly in their heightened investment in local identity; but they also instituted a new and perilous *illusio*, in which artistic autonomy (pure painting) coexisted uneasily with political patronage. Moreover, the popular success of the new museums and the feverish coverage of new Spanish artists in the press gave rise to charges of consumerism. Arguing that such nationalist or localist sponsorship is sometimes 'counterproductive', Emma Dent Coad writes that 'in Spain today, art is publicly seen as an item of consumption, a highbrow elitist activity where connoisseurs, intellectuals, and patrons mingle' (Coad 1995: 375). Interestingly, Coad contradicts her own 'highbrow' hypothesis, citing 'coverage in the gossip magazine *Hola* of the Thyssen entourage', whose Madrid museum opened in 1992. The gallery and the supermarket thus merged in the tabloid press; and state sponsorship coincided with (in Burgin's phrase) the 'roar of fashion'. With the genesis of an impure aesthetic, artists, suddenly celebrities, struggled to combine the long-term logic of production with newly accelerated and facilitated conditions of distribution.

In Spain, as in the USA, the critical evaluation of such conditions took many forms. Writing in the late 1980s, a consecrated art historian such as Francisco Calvo Serraller charts repeated waves of artistic innovation from the 'new imagination' after Franco (including once more such personal figurative painters as Pérez Villalta and Barceló) to the 'new generation for a new time' which lives and works 'beyond Spain' (1988: 165, 173). Tracking trends in the most traditionalist art-historical manner ('conceptual, minimalist, neo-abstract, neo-figurative'), Calvo nevertheless suggests some contradictions in the national art scene. Thus, while 'Spanishness' has, he claims, been the 'principal theme of contemporary Spanish art since the 19th century', unlike in the case of other nations, no 'Spanish school' was thought to exist in art history, leading to the paradox that the nation that produced Picasso, Gris and Miró was held to have no 'distinguishing marks' (9–10). And if the 'new model of the artist in democratic Spain' is 'cosmopolitan, well informed

... dynamic' (162), the public promotion of young art abroad is 'scattered' and 'contradictory' (177). There is thus no correspondence between what Spanish art specialists take to be most representative of their country and what is officially displayed at the Venice Biennale. Moreover, the artists chosen for 'New Images of Spain' at the New York Guggenheim in 1980 (claimed by Calvo to be 'a new generation who change the panorama' (181)), do not coincide with the 'Five Spanish Artists' also shown in New York at the Artists Space just five years later (178). In Bourdieu's terms, there is no correspondence between competing hierarchies: external (social success) and internal (peer consecration).

Perhaps the most symbolically charged of times and locations was the massive group exhibition of some fifty contemporary Spanish artists staged in the central patio of the Spanish pavilion at the 1992 World's Fair in Seville. Rarely could the contradictions posed by the state institutionalization of the avant-garde have been posed more acutely. In the introduction to the catalogue, which was graced by a soft-focus portrait of their Majesties the King and Queen in formal dress, academic art critic and poet José Luis Brea rereads the spatial and temporal dislocations of the postmodern in a specifically Spanish context, adopting a metaphorical language that could not be further from Calvo's dogged descriptions. The title 'Passages' is borrowed from Benjamin. Suggesting both a peripheral space, in which there can be no centre, and an ephemeral time, in which there can be no singular history, it asks the gallery's audience to take pleasure in fragments and ruins, labyrinths and 'broken, local, precise, instantaneous places' (17). But Benjamin's 'passages' are, of course, commercial arcades, icons of, and refuges from, urban alienation. And Brea also invokes, here at the World's Fair, the now inevitable commercialization of artistic practice: 'Where better' to see art, argues Brea, 'than the place which is not separate from life?' (18). Exploiting and benefiting from 'the fascination of the showcase', art takes up its place 'behind the plate glass [amongst] implacable homologated objects, submitted to ultimate equivalence'. Reduced to commodities, art objects participate none the less in the seduction of the marketplace that, in a reverse movement, 'possesses man . . . in consumerism'. How long, asks Brea, can 'art bear . . . this banal challenge of its contaminated phase – that of inhabiting the passage, the high altar of goods?'

If art, irrevocably impure, has 'in the passages . . . abandoned its autonomous form' (20), and if topicality is 'untimely' ('set by the rhythms of the market and the artistic industry' (21)), still Brea is canny about the role of states, in the hands of 'image advisors', as 'accomplices to this chaos, this delirium' (19). And the history of Spanish museums in the same period reveals that just as there can be no absolute master when anomie is institutionalized (the fifty artists of the Pavilion are wholly heterogeneous), so there can be no master discourse of nationality in the contested, broken terrain of art production and distribution. Thus, as Trinidad Manchado has written, the 'unprecedented number of public spaces dedicated to modern and contemporary art [that] opened in Spain' during the PSOE's rule (1982–96) coincided not only with the international art market boom, but with 'a national drive to reinvent [Spain] as a modern country', in which 'contemporary culture becomes a highly valued commodity and museums . . . some of the best stages for the performance of this new dynamic Spanish identity' (Manchado 2000: 92). Yet the creation of the Reina Sofía in 1986 proved rather the impossibility of 'building a coherent national collection of modern art' (93): political intrusion was frequent; the representative nature of the permanent collection was challenged; and the first director's attempt to take his purchasing policy 'against the market, against ARCO' (92) proved disastrous. Its success lying rather, as Manchado notes, in its high-calibre temporary shows, the massive and monumental Reina Sofía reveals rather the dislocation and impermanence, the inability to separate art and commerce, lamented and celebrated in Brea's 'passages'.

The intrusiveness of Barcelona's MACBA, a sleek glass structure inserted into the still impoverished heart of the urban Raval or Barrio Chino, also drew controversy, as did its exhibition policy. But Valencia's IVAM is generally held to be the most successful of the new museums. Avoiding to some extent the pitfalls of political patronage, IVAM has (according to Selma Reuben Holo) struck 'the appropriate balance between the local and the global, the old and the new' (1997: 319). Split emblematically between two sites, the medieval convent of the Centre del Carmé and the modernist structure named for Catalan sculptor Julio González, the IVAM has focused its purchasing policy on specialist areas (such as abstraction of the 1930s). Freed from the impossible burden of representing the contested nation-state, it has also been able to forge cultural links in its temporary exhibitions between Valencian and international artists, with successful shows ranging from Warhol to the active local community. In its basement IVAM displays the ruins of the medieval walls on which it is built. More perhaps than any other Spanish art insitution, it reveals the critical potential of those 'broken, local, and precise places' celebrated in Brea's postmodern passages.

7 Miquel Barceló, *L'amour fou* (1984), mixed media on canvas.
Collection of Contemporary Art Fundación 'La Caixa', Barcelona.
© ADAGP, Paris and DACS, London 2002.

Barceló: the signature

> The new Spain is visually hot and its artists are fast becoming interna-
> tional stars . . . Riding high this year [is] Miquel Barceló . . . Last year the
> thirty year old Barceló dominated Madrid. His vaguely punk look, his
> showman style, his 'savage' art – born of rock, Baroque, poster art,
> comics, and a dose of New York School abstraction – suit the mood.
>
> (Probst Solomon 1987: unnumbered, 121)

Miquel Barceló seems to embody the reduction of the signature
'Spanish artist' to the single value of celebrity. Covering his recent
solo show at the Reina Sofía, *El Mundo* wrote that he 'has become a
phenomenon comparable only to some film or sports stars', and
cited Picasso in the art world and Almodóvar in cinema as reference
points (Sierra 1999). The website of the Bilbao Guggenheim claims
Barceló as 'the greatest example of precocity in Spanish art', noting
that his first 'scandal' ('necessary to any artist thirsty for glory') was
in 1973 at age seventeen, when he exhibited in his native Mallorca

8 Miquel Barceló, *Taula dibuixada* (1991), mixed media on canvas.
Collection of Contemporary Art Fundación 'La Caixa', Barcelona.
© ADAGP, Paris and DACS, London 2002.

boxes of decomposing organic matter, now displayed in the Palma
Museum (Guggenheim 2000).[1] For the Guggenheim, Barceló's career
is marked (like Burgin's gyrating toy) by sheer velocity: beginning
'at a gallop', he 'at once' set off for Barcelona, where, allied with
designer Javier Mariscal, he became 'the spearhead of the wild youths
(*jóvenes salvajes*)', compared to Francesco Clemente's Italian trans-
vanguard. Then came in swift succession his European launch at
the prestigious Documenta group show in Kassel (1982), 'his studio
in Paris, his journeys through Africa, a great deal of money, and,
like any successful artist, furious enemies, hoping to see him fail as
soon as possible'.[2] Barceló himself has proclaimed his impatience

9 Miquel Barceló, *Six figues xines* (1997), mixed media on canvas.
Collection of Contemporary Art Fundación 'La Caixa', Barcelona.
© ADAGP, Paris and DACS, London 2002.

with the prolonged artistic apprenticeship that was expected of him
when he arrived in Barcelona: he was not willing to begin as a 'bell
boy and rise in seniority by degrees' (Calvo Serraller 1988: 162). It
is for this reason that Calvo consecrated him the 'emblematic' figure
of the 1980s, the 'new model of the artist in democratic Spain'.

The Guggenheim's symptomatically compressed and accelerated
biography omits some institutional aspects of a career that is still
attacked for the supposed immediacy and facility of its success even
after twenty years of continuous production. Thus Barceló was represented by Bruno Bischofberger in Europe (first solo exhibition in
Zurich 1984) and by Leo Castelli in uptown New York (first solo

1986). Barceló thus joined the elite company of US artists represented by Castelli: Jasper Johns, Roy Lichtenstein, Robert Rauschenberg and Frank Stella (artincontext 2000). Compared by Spanish critics in 1985 to Baselitz, Clemente and Schnabel (Guasch 1997: 338), he is now held with those same foreign artists in La Caixa's Barcelona Contemporary Art Collection (lacaixa 2000),[3] and with lesser Spanish stars Pérez Villalta and Iglesias in the Fundación March's Museu d'Art Espanyol Contemporani in Palma, Mallorca. Supported by the most prestigious private commissions, Barceló has also profited from state subvention: he was one of the 'Five Spanish Artists' in the New York exhibition of 1985 subsidized by the Foreign Affairs Section of the Ministry of Culture, and one of the many included in the 1992 World's Fair. Representing both Catalonia and Spain to themselves and to their others, Barceló has shown at the IVAM (1995), and has most recently been awarded major retrospectives at both Barcelona's MACBA and Madrid's Reina Sofía. Definitive (if localist) institutionalization has also arrived with the joint establishment by the artist, the town council of Artà, and the University of the Balearic Islands of a personal foundation: the 'Fons documental Miquel Barceló'. Collecting press files, catalogues, audiovisual material, posters and 'photographs of the artist's activity' but, as yet, no actual graphic works, the Foundation claims with pride that Barceló, famously nomadic, is 'resident' in Artà (uib 2000).

The reference to photographs in the foundation's collection is significant. Central to Barceló's mythic career has been his collaboration with photographer Jean Marie del Moral, who for eight years documented Barceló at work in such diverse locations as Paris, Barcelona, Mali and Majorca before producing a documentary distributed by Franco-German television: *Les Ateliers de Barceló* (1992) (lasept-arte 2000). Intense, brooding and often stripped to the waist, looming large over splattered canvases that are placed on the ground, Barceló has thus benefited from what has been called 'the extreme fetishization of the actual moment of creation' (Haywood 1988: 8). It is a fetishization that is characteristic, yet problematic, in the media representation of contemporary artists, and one that feeds on stereotypes of a 'typically Spanish nature': 'the image of instinct, fierceness, and a heated expressivity with classical touches' (Blanch 1992: 24).

Barceló's career would thus seem to be an extreme case of the 'end game' of impure painting, of the interpenetration of art and money. Indeed, in spite of a notoriously anti-social temperament, Barceló was photographed in New York with Warhol[4] (whom he has professed greatly to admire), and in Europe secured the support of celebrities such as Parisian author and socialite Hervé Guibert, who penned a book on him (Guibert 1993). In Bourdieu's terms, Barceló's 'art of living' is singular indeed. Indifferent to politics and morality (professing in one early interview to have made more money from drug running than painting (Espaliú and Paneque [1984] 1986: 450)), Barceló combines the economic logic of the artistic industry with the symbolic capital of aesthetic renown, once held to be mutually exclusive. Thus Spanish academics, while helping to promote a career that coincided with the return to painting and 'new figuration' at home and abroad, have not hesitated to proclaim Barceló's artistic, rather than financial, value. In a book with the significant title 'From the Future to the Past', Calvo praises Barceló's 'symbolic gravity', sourced in the masters of the Prado and grounded in a 'historicism' that is truly 'contemporary' (1988: 165–6). Barceló, he writes, 'drags' history behind him. Writing three years earlier on Barceló's 'trail' (*rastro*, another significantly physical term), Calvo invokes Tintoretto to explain the luminosity of Barceló's recent paintings on such learned subjects as the Louvre, the cinema and the library ([1985] 1990: 362). Barceló is not only 'a new type of personality'; he is also 'the most highly rated (*acreditado*) Spanish painter' (365). In a contemporary interview with conceptualist Pepe Espaliú (a somewhat unlikely interlocutor), Barceló rejected the 'savage' label with which he had been branded, claiming that if he placed the canvas on the ground like Jackson Pollock, for him Pollock and Tintoretto were 'almost the same' (Espaliú and Paneque [1984] 1986: 451). Likewise, in an introductory essay to a facsimile of Barceló's sketch book of the same year, Sergio Vila-San-Juan does not merely make the now customary reference to Barceló's photographic image at the moment of creation ('he looks like he is going to smash the photographer's face in'); he also claims that Barceló's 'dense, potent brushstrokes' labour in 'the landscape of art history' (Vila-San-Juan 1984: unnumbered). Barceló's signature citations, then, are not the post-historicism of ironic pastiche, but rather a newly contemporaneous engagement with the past, invoking, in its abandon and singularity, the aesthetic rebellions of the nineteenth century.[5]

The paintings chosen for 'Five Spanish Artists' (all from 1984) reveal this grand aspiration to mastery of vision and division. Large-format, mixed technique works (200 × 300 cms), they revisit the lost sites and genres of artistic consecration. *Tinta, vino, lluvia* shows the painter asleep in the studio, his table awash in coloured fluids; *Bibliothèque de la mer* offers dark, brooding books beneath the waves; *Vanitatis circus* is a monumental still life in which soup, fruit and red wine spill over an open book; finally *Cala Marsal* is a landscape of an indigo inlet, snaking towards the spectator.[6] In these ambitious paintings, whose richly textured oil paint is intermittently embedded with collage, Barceló recuperates the self-portrait, the still life and the landscape. But, as Ramón Tío Belido notes in his introduction to the catalogue, Barceló's very loaded Parisian locations (the Louvre, the library and the studio) also reveal their painter's 'direct connection with his environment', as places, respectively, of abstraction, know-ledge and action (Tío Belido 1985: 30, 28). Denying the Spanishness of Barceló's work ('Barceló does not know Spain; nor Spain him'), Tío Belido asserts the 'singularity' of his struggle to 'make tangible the implicit relationship between subject and artist' (23, 24).

This rigorous self-examination (so characteristic of autonomous art, pure painting and the haunting memory of modernism) was less visible to US commentators mesmerized by Spanish exceptionalism. At their most banal, they submitted whole-heartedly to the roar of fashion: 'The new Spain', wrote *Artnews* in September 1987, 'abounds in a most un-European optimism: its government is run by young Socialists from Seville who resemble bull fighters and rock stars more than politicians' (Probst Solomon 1987: 121). Between languid strolls and late lunches ('gesture is what counts'), the reporter breezes through Barceló ('whose show last winter at New York's Leo Castelli gallery was widely praised') and hyperrealist Antonio López ('who took New York by storm in his Marlborough show last season') (121, 124). Unselfconsciously conflating Barceló's 'savage' contem-poraneity with López's archaizing academicism ('he truly sees Spain – a country stuffed with bits and pieces of the 19th century' (124)), she claims that Spain is 'drenched in visual sensibility' (121).

But reports soon become more nuanced. A feature in the same month's *Art in America* was already canny on state support and international relations: due in part to an 'activist' Ministry of Cul-ture, 'for the first time since Franco's death Spanish artists have the opportunity to participate fully in the art world mainstream' (Gambrell 1987: 160). And beyond Barceló's local reputation for 'media hype', *AA* baptized him 'a serious painter', even if it found his 'self-conscious symbolism' in such pictures as the library series inconsistent with his supposed sunny 'Mediterranean sensibility' (163). By 1989 *Artnews*'s Spanish round-up could begin with the role of art in urban planning (the conversion of convents to galleries in Barcelona, Seville and Valencia), as well as the continuing 'enthu-siastic support' of the Ministry of Culture for young artists abroad (Cembalest 1989: 128). And it shrewdly pointed to the source of Barceló's 'mystique' in his synthesis of diverse chronological and geographical elements: 'his ability to seem classical, provincial, and up to date at the same time' (129). Such a blend coincided not with an implicitly unchanging Spanish or Mediterranean 'sensibility', but rather with current conditions in the global artistic industries: 'The market for a post-Franco art that is both provincial and international is beckoning . . . [There now exist] outlets and support [that were] impossible just ten years ago' (129). To put it in Bourdieu's terms once more, the subjective dispositions of Barceló, Mallorcan resident and global nomad, thus coincided magically with the objective conditions of the market, which sought an art that was at once exotic and familiar, classical and contemporary. As early as 1986, Castelli would sell a Barceló painting for over $100,000 (Cembalest 1989: 129).

Barceló: two exhibitions

> Criticism, caught up in the web of dealers, gallery owners, politicians, and institutions . . . has displaced history . . . Exhibitions [are a kind of] anthropology [an] instrument for the diffusion, refinement, and even gestation [of art].
>
> (Guasch 1997: 15–16)

If, as Bourdieu's sociology teaches us, art is irrevocably impure, how can we account for the intense subjective experience of painting? And how can we reinsert the individual painter into the artistic field? One vehicle for this process is the exhibition, which is at once subjective experience (for painter and visitor) and objective institution (for owner and sponsor). Anna Maria Guasch offers a valuable commentary on Spanish art of the 1980s in her detailed accounts of group exhibitions. Thus the ironically named 'Madrid D. F.' in 1980 (at the Museo Municipal in Madrid) marked the new figurative painters' break with the more theoretical conceptualists of the 1970s (Guasch 1997: 337); while 'Cota Cero sobre el nivel del mar' in 1985 (at the Caja de Ahorros in Alicante) was the show that promoted Barceló, Pérez Villalta and artist-architect Tomás Navarro Baldeweg as Spanish counterparts to Baselitz, Clemente and Schnabel (338). 'Al ras' (1991) at the Caixa in Barcelona marked the 'crisis of modernity' and minimalism in twelve 'unaffiliated' artists; while 'Anys 90: distància zero' (at the Santa Mònica, Barcelona) was a 'chaotic' show, exhibiting no fewer than forty-five artists (338).

Barceló's career at once coincided with, and distanced itself from, these collective tendencies. While initially benefiting from the 'battle in favour of painting' identified by Guasch at the beginning of the decade, Barceló did not participate in the process of purification or divestment of resources suggested by the titles of these trend-setting shows. Indeed, after reclaiming self-depiction, landscapes and still lifes in the early 1980s, Barceló mastered the new genre of portraits and the new medium of ceramics. Moreover, US art magazines of the 1990s increasingly granted Barceló the status of a consecrated artist of the pure aesthetic, outside the contemporary chaos. *Artnews*'s review of ten new mixed media paintings at Castelli praised Barceló as a 'master draftsman who sketches wet-into-wet gouache over conté crayon' (Moorman 1990); while *Art International* in the same year acclaimed him as one of 'Spanish Art's New Heirs Apparent' who had 'shift[ed] attention from autobiographical, existential concerns to cover timely subjects including the weight of history, the march of time, and the celebrity of the artist' (Combalia 1990: 54). A further show at Castelli in 1993 ('a baroque celebration of natural order and decay') led *Art in America* to write that Barceló's 'disintegrating still lifes' revealed the 'plenitude not of harvest but of death and decay' in 'virtuoso brushwork and pulsating compositions scaled like 19th century history paintings' (Heartney 1993); while *Artnews*'s account of a show of portraits at Bischofberger's Zurich gallery in 1995 praised Barceló's 'powers of perception' and 'distinctive treatment of technique': paint is 'torn, distressed, pleated' to achieve a 'raw emotional edge' (Krienke 1995). Versatile and virtuoso (almost 'insulting' in his technical facility (MACBA 1998: 27)), Barceló thus began to treat big issues in ambitious formats at the same time that most contemporary art, caught in the 'end game' of disenchantment, divested itself of such heroic ambitions. Barceló's dazzling expertise in draftmanship also meant that he rejected the 'klutzy smear' typical of such wilfully naive painting as that of Clemente.

   The catalogues of two recent retrospectives present Barceló's career as highly coherent in its diversity, by no means as chaotic as the narratives of the Spanish national art scene. Unsurprisingly, perhaps, they also seek to incorporate Barceló in nationalist contexts, a location which, I will argue, he eludes through the logic of the 'passage', mentioned above. 'Miquel Barceló 1987–97' was an exhibition of some 200 mixed media paintings and ceramics organized by, and held at, the MACBA from 3 April to 21 June 1998. John S. Zvereff, the acting director of the museum (whose 'President' Jordi Pujol also leads the Generalitat) identifies the artist and his (presumed) home territory: it is ten years since Barceló last had a major show in the city and this retrospective will initiate a series of solo shows by Catalan artists (MACBA 1998: 8). Curator Pep Subirós pursues the analogy: 'Barceló, Barcelona' in 1987 had been held in the former theatre of the old Casa de la Caritat. In the intervening decade Barceló's artistic ambitions have paralleled Barcelona's enviable cultural achievements: the rehabilitated ruins of the Casa now hold the Centre de Cultura Contemporània; on what was an abandoned lot, strewn with trash, now rises the MACBA building (13). Barceló, resident in the city only from 1976 to 1982, will no longer 'escape' its proud citizens.

Subirós runs through Barceló's career as a series of locations: his close but problematic engagement with the cultural legacy of the Mediterranean (15); his 'universalization' of an Africa which is not exotic or idyllic, but rather 'a search for uncertainty' (18); his continuing 'exploration of new territories, new media' (29). The layout of the catalogue also facilitates this narrativization of time and space: 'biographical notes' for discrete periods (1957–87, 1998–92, 1993–7) precede the works themselves, which are interspersed with selections from Barceló's sketch books and journals, and critical essays by famous foreign scholars such as John Berger. The overall effect is that of a life dedicated to pure painting: Subirós claims that Barceló's great theme is the 'integration of art and life' (15); Bernard Goy compares Barceló's lengthy sojourns in Africa to those of Rimbaud (61); Barceló himself contemplates the all too material subjects of his painting in Mali ('split animal heads, ants, and scorpions'), and dismisses the 'cynical exercises [of artists] with one hand on the telephone and one on *Art Forum*' (83). If painters should avoid the roar of fashion, however, they should also resist the lure of public commissions: 'To be an artist in the West you must above all not even walk down streets near the Ministries of Culture' (87).

Indifferent to the financial comforts of the art market (he falls seriously ill in the 50 degree heat of Dogon), Barceló also takes on the heavy, even deadly, burden of art history. In an address at the Prado, he tells a parable of a guard trapped in the museum as it is being fumigated (mysterious worms are devouring the canvases). He dies in agony before a Tintoretto (MACBA 1998: 130). This 'Pradoxismo' not only confirms Barceló's engagement with past masters; it also suggests his quest for spontaneous gestures beyond historical reflection: many of his own African sketches will be made in a sketch book left in a termite nest, the resulting random holes giving rise to bodies, cavities and animals worked in gouache.[7] A master of both colour and tone (the richly saturated Mediterranean works giving way to starkly monochrome African landscapes), Barceló also turns his hand to texture: sticking found objects into his rich impasto, layering paint over grains of rice, staining the canvas or paper with mud, fruit or octopus ink. And as the paintings grow larger, so the themes become more transcendental: *De rerum natura* (1992; 300 × 400 cm) is a swirling sea-green mass of plants, fish and birds engulfing an inverted, eviscerated donkey; *Setze penjats* (1992; 155 × 967 cm) shows sixteen animal carcasses up against the picture plane, inverted once more, traced in black on a ground of bilious yellow and above a blood-red band, strewn with skulls and fruit. Typically, however, the iconographic reference to the Crucifixion is undercut by literalist localism: Barceló claims that in Mallorca slaughtered animals are bled by being hung on lines in this way (MACBA 1998: 26).

An even larger retrospective at the Reina Sofía ('Miquel Barceló: obra sobre papel 1979–99'), which ran from 14 September to 21 November 1999, confines itself to works on paper (including the celebrated termite works, which continue to evolve after the painter's intervention). Here too Barceló's extraterritorial ambitions are held in check: in his introduction, the current Minister of Education and Culture from the Partido Popular claims Barceló as 'one of the most notable figures in contemporary Spanish art' (Reina Sofía 1999: 13), while the director, José Guirao, reminds us that Barceló's first exhibition in a public museum was at Madrid's Palacio de Velásquez in 1985 (15). Co-sponsored by the Caja de Ahorros of Granada (yet another Spanish savings bank which invests in contemporary art), the exhibition will take this 'emblematic artist of the Spain of the transition [to democracy]' on tour to Granada, São Paolo, Montevideo and Tel Aviv.

But Barceló himself also explores the nature of Spanishness. Just as the inside cover of the MACBA catalogue shows a sixteenth-century *mapa mundi*, plotting the Spanish discoveries, customized with Barceló's typically lavish flood of blue ink, so the Reina Sofía showed a 'Carte d'Espagne' (1990; 73 × 100 cm), an anamorphically stretched peninsula, parched white and studded with textured mounds like the African landscapes (212–13). It is a study for the backdrop of Barceló's production design for Falla's operatic sketch *El retablo de Maese Pedro* (Opéra Comique, Paris), in which the Cervantine characters were all clothed by Barceló in shimmering insect carapaces. Rejecting local identities and political patronage, Barceló nevertheless reworks in typically idiosyncratic and inventive forms the cartographic and cultural fetishes of the nation-state. Decentred, displaced and undomesticated, however, such places become, rather, passages: as ephemeral and fragile as insect wings.

Combining the singular (and disinterested) art of living of Bourdieu's nineteenth-century rebel with the charismatic celebrity of the contemporary artistic industrialist, Barceló thus replaces fixed territories with flexible passages, singular histories with multiple moments.

In defence of autonomy

Painting has gradually given up all its attributes one by one until it's only skin and bone . . . For many years I've thought that it's very good to count on all the possibilities of painting: depth, space, representation, narrative; to try to retrieve everything, if only as a provocation.

(Barceló, quoted in Reina Sofía 1999: 32)

It was the Reina Sofía exhibition of an 'intimate and unshown' Barceló that inspired comparisons of the artist at age forty-two to a film or sport celebrity (Sierra 1999). And we are told by *El Mundo* that Barceló does not mind being treated like a star 'once a year': the retrospective was opened with a glamorous party at a 'glitzy hall' in the heart of the Retiro, an event curiously out of sync with the works themselves: fragile pieces of paper, gnawed by insects, stained by earth, rolled and folded by Barceló in the course of his global travels.

But if this exhibition seemed to mark the definitive consecration of Barceló's social success, *El Mundo* still remarked that Reina Sofía's permanent holdings, supposedly the national collection of contemporary art, featured only one work by the artist, and that was inherited from its unloved and unvisited predecessor, the Museo Español de Arte Contemporáneo. Barceló's position thus remains fragile. Commercial renown can still threaten the accumulation of long-term symbolic capital (as the Reina Sofía's ambivalent attitude shows). Conversely, a selfless devotion to pure painting can damage commercial health. Barceló's flight to Africa in search of new inspiration could not have been guaranteed to bring success: indeed, it led to a lengthy hiatus in which he produced only small-scale, modest works. The contrast with his Italian counterpart Francesco Clemente, whose sojourns in India have produced decorative (and saleable) exotic and erotic imagery, is telling. Moreover, in spite of his intermittent attraction to subjects that reconfirm 'savage' preconceptions of Spanishness (including a series on the *corrida*), Barceló, the famous figurativist, has a tendency towards abstraction. The monochrome paintings of mysterious cavities stirred by poles recall Pollock; the glaucous 'soups' blur into non-representational feasts of fierce brush-work, worthy of the purest of abstract expressionists.[8] In his constant concern for surface and painterly gesture, in his continuing rigorous self-examination, Barceló coincides with Greenberg's prescriptions for pure painting. But while the art market gives high prices to such masters as Rothko, on the contemporary scene such high-mindedness is hardly the dominant fashion. The young British artists who successfully provoked the 'battle of Brooklyn' specialize in conceptual jokes and factitious media controversy. It is a parade that one respected British commentator has recently called 'a relentless litany of self-abuse' (Searle 2000).

Spaniards tend, understandably, to exaggerate the foreign success of their native sons; indeed, the curator of the Reina Sofía exhibition, Enrique Juncosa, claims that Barceló's local celebrity is the result of the excessive attention to foreign favour at the time of the transition, 'when this country stopped being part of the Third World' (Sierra 1999). While I have documented Barceló's considerable commercial and artistic success in the US market and magazines, he remains relatively little known in a UK whose insular media remain in thrall to the roar of fashion: a spot check at the book shops of the major British museums reveals not one copy of a Barceló catalogue, in spite of numerous volumes devoted to his US and European rivals.

For all his nomadism and celebrity, Barceló's work is to be seen within the context of Spanish (and Catalan or Mallorcan) respect for high art. The summer season crowned by Barceló's Madrid retrospective was characterized by major exhibitions devoted to what Spaniards call 'the historical avant-gardes' (Manrique 1999) and an extraordinary expansion of public and private sponsorship for both classical and contemporary art. Thus it was announced that the ambitious new extension to the Prado would be opened a year earlier than planned, in 2003 (*La Razón* 1999), and that the extension of the Thyssen Museum would be completed in 2002 (Romero 1999). The Ministry of Culture sought an annex for the Museo de Sorolla in Madrid (Pulido 1999), while the Museu Picasso in Barcelona celebrated the completion of its expansion in October 1999 (Spiegel 1999). The Reina Sofía itself commissioned a new extension from French avant-gardist Jean Nouvel, who had most recently created the Musée de la Publicité in the ever-expanding Louvre (Samaniego 1999).

Continuing a welcome shift from metropolis to periphery, initiated by changes in cultural funding since the transition (Hooper 1995: 324), even Galicia, the most impoverished and underdeveloped autonomous region, invested in ambitious contemporary projects: an Island of Sculpture featuring twelve international artists off Pontevedra (Carbajo 1999) and a City of Culture costing eighteen billion pesetas burrowed into a hill opposite Santiago's ancient city centre (Hermida 1999). The first project was said to 'fill a gap in the contemporary artistic heritage (*patrimonio*) which the city was suffering'; the second was commissioned from New York deconstructivist Peter Eisenmann. Rarely have the respect for art, the quest for modernity, and the pursuit of internationalism been conjugated so clearly. Back in Valencia, however, the Generalitat attempted to impose a massive sculpture at the entrance to the IVAM. Administrators and artists (including Barceló) vigorously opposed this attack on artistic 'independence' (Bono 2000).

Barceló had made his clearest bid for transcendence yet in his most symbolically charged studio: the ruined church of Santa Eulalia dei Catalani in Palermo (Barceló 1998). Barceló hung a 'Christ-Mandrake' over the high altar, and, in the chapels, studies of men bent under the burden of a bicycle or beasts hung upside down from a tree of death. Piled terracotta skulls lined the aisles, and severed heads of men and beasts were scratched on the walls, whose rough texture echoed both Barceló's own impasto and the caves of Altamira. The historical references are significant. For if Barceló's intervention was necessarily temporary and provisional (seen only between 17 October and 13 December 1998), still it powerfully combined both the Mediterranean legacy and the African experience that have framed his career. Indeed, the civic sponsors of the exhibition claimed that it truly engaged in a maritime history more evoked than enacted, renewing traditional connections between Palermo and Barcelona, Palermo and Palma. They even cite the twin 'roads to freedom' of Spain after Franco and (more hopefully) Sicily after the Mafia (unpaginated). Far from the art supermarket with its 'high altar of goods', the abandoned church, both ruin and labyrinth, is thus the final example of Brea's 'passage', marginal and provisional, and of Berger's definition of Barceló's 'place': a space in which an event will or has taken place (MACBA 1998: 174).

Bourdieu argues for the continuing cogency of intellectual autonomy, now under threat with the increasing interpenetration of art and money ([1992] 1996: 344). Scholars need not bow to the demands of the marketplace that quick reading and writing (or 'thoughtless thought' (346)) be the only standards of value. Similarly, I have argued that Barceló proves the continuing potency of autonomous art or pure painting, however compromised they may be by the irrevocable claims of commerce. To unveil the *illusio* (the necessary complicity of artist and audience) is not to destroy the astonished pleasure, even love, I felt at the richness of Barceló's art as I traversed the many rooms of the MACBA and the Reina Sofía. Rather, it is further to appreciate the singularity of Barceló's appeal to colour and texture, of his representations and citations, even as he takes up his place within an artistic field in which works, producers and institutions are inseparable and mutually constituting.[9]

Notes

1 Barceló's attitude to Mallorca is ambivalent. In an early interview, in 1984, he compared himself to 'centrifugal' Mallorcans, historical exiles or heretics such as Ramón Llull (MACBA 1998: 12).

2 Pep Subirós's excellent introductory essay to the MACBA exhibition is called 'Out of Africa' ('Regreso de Africa') (MACBA 1998: 11–29), thereby suggesting the centrality of the African experience to Barceló's career. Subirós reads Barceló's career as a vital but 'impossible project', one that reasserts the ambitions of 'all great artists' (29).

3 One of the avowed objects of the Caixa's collection is 'to integrate and relate contemporary Spanish art into the international context' (lacaixa 2000). These transnational ambitions, parallel to those of Barceló himself, are also illustrated by the only work shown on the website: Richard Long's *Catalan Circle* (1986), an intricate mosaic of indigenous rocks placed on the Foundations's floor by the British land artist.

4 Spain has its own tradition of pop art, but one which, unlike Warhol, is (as Marko Daniel argues) intrinsically political (Sainsbury Centre 1998: 30).

5 Like Pep Subirós, Hervé Landry argues for the necessary 'failure' of Barceló's heroic and impossible project (MACBA 1998: 249), a failure which does not of course prevent him from comparing Barceló with past masters such as Pollock.

6 The polyglot ambitions of Barceló's titles are echoed by those of his journal, which is frequently written in French (see the substantial extracts in MACBA 1998 and Reina Sofía 1999). Barceló contrasts the terse monosyllables of Mallorquí Catalan with the elegant formality of French (Reina Sofía 1999: 286).

7 Enrique Juncosa claims that the sketch book and the drawing are characteristic media of Barceló's nomadic career, permitting as they do autobiographical confession and spontaneous execution (Reina Sofía 1999: 19).

8 Barceló claims characteristically that what fascinates him in Old Masters is the surface texture: brush or human hairs embedded in the varnish (Reina Sofía 1999: 287).

9 For a definition of the field, following Bourdieu, see Smith 2000: 76, 77, 81.

References

Anon. (2000) Fall Auction Fever. *Art in America*, January, pp. 25, 27.
artincontext (2000) www.artincontext.org/new_york/leo_castelli_gallery_uptown. Consulted 22 February.
Barceló, Miquel (1998) *Il Cristo della Vucciria*, Milan: Charta.
Blanch, María Teresa (1992) 1982–1992: Spain at the Beginning of a Well-Defined Intersection. In *Pasajes: Spanish Art Today*, Seville: Pabellón de España/Electa, pp. 23–32.
Bono, Ferrán (2000) La Generalitat rectifica y acepta debatir la ubicación de la escultura impuesta al IVAM. *El País*, 21 March.
Bourdieu, Pierre ([1992] 1996) *The Rules of Art: Genesis and Structure of the Literary Field*, Cambridge: Polity.
Brea, José Luis (1992) Passages. In *Pasajes: Spanish Art Today*, Seville: Pabellón de España/Electa, pp. 17–22.
Burgin, Victor (1986) *The End of Art Theory: Criticism and Postmodernity*. London: Macmillan.
Calvo Serraller, Francisco (1988) *Del futuro al pasado: vanguardia y tradición*. Madrid: Alianza.
—— ([1985] 1990) El rastro de Miquel Barceló. In *Pintores españoles entre dos fines de siglo (1880–1990): De Eduardo Rosales a Miquel Barceló*, Madrid: Alianza, pp. 361–7.
Carbajo, Primitivo (1999) 12 artistas crean en Pontevedra una Isla de Esculturas. *El País*, 29 July.
Cembalest, Robin (1989) Learning to Absorb the Shock of the New. *Artnews*, September, pp. 127–31.
Coad, Emma Dent (1995) Artistic Patronage and Enterprise Culture. In Helen Graham and Jo Labanyi (eds), *Spanish Cultural Studies: An Introduction*, Oxford: Oxford University Press, pp. 373–6.
Combalia, Victoria (1990) A Love–Hate Relationship: Spanish Art's New Heirs Apparent'. *Art International*, Winter, pp. 50–6.
Danto, Arthur C. (1997) *After the End of Art: Contemporary Art and the Pale of History*. Princeton: Princeton University Press.
Dubin, Steven C. (2000) How 'Sensation' Became a Scandal. *Art in America*, January, pp. 53–5, 57, 59.
Ebony, David (2000) Pittsburgh Cultural District Takes Shape. *Art in America*, March, p. 39.
Hermida, Xosé (1999) Peter Eisenman construirá en Santiago una Ciudad de la Cultura de 18.000 millones. *El País*, 28 August.
Espaliú, P. and Paneque, G. ([1984] 1986) Miquel Barceló [interview]. In Simón Marchán Fiz, *Del arte objetual al arte de concepto*, Madrid: Akal, pp. 450–1.
Esterow, Milton (1999) Sick Stuff? An Open Letter to Mayor Giuliani. *Artnews*, November, p. 208.
Five Spanish Artists [catalogue] (1985) New York: Artists Space.

Gambrell, Jamey (1987) Five from Spain. *Art in America*, September, pp. 160–71.

Guasch, Anna Maria (1997) *El arte del siglo XX en sus exposiciones, 1945–95*. Barcelona: Serbal.

Guggenheim (2000) Miquel Barceló; www.larioja.com/guggenheim/museo/barcelo.htm. Consulted 29 February.

Guibert, Hervé (1993) *L'Homme au chapeau rouge*. Paris: Gallimard.

Haywood, Philip (1988) Introduction: Echoes and Reflections: The Representation of Representations. In *Media Representations of Visual Art and Artists*, London and Paris: John Libbey, pp. 1–25.

Heartney, Eleanor (1993) Miquel Barceló at Leo Castelli. *Art in America*, February, p. 105.

Hickey, David (2000) Clemente: Solomon R. Guggenheim Museum, New York. *Artforum*, January, p. 107.

Holo, Selma Reuben (1997) The Art Museum as a Means of Refiguring Regional Identity in Democratic Spain. In Marsha Kinder (ed.), *Refiguring Spain: Cinema/Media/Representation*, Durham, NC, and London: Duke University Press, pp. 301–26.

Hooper, John (1995) *The New Spaniards*. London: Penguin.

Krienke, Mary (1995) Miquel Barceló. Bruno Bischofberger. Zurich. *Artnews*, December, p. 159.

lacaixa (2000) www.lacaixa.es/fundacio/eng/ambits/arts/colart.htm%espanyols. Consulted 29 February.

lasept-arte (2000) *Les Ateliers de Barceló*: TV/Video Rights; www.lasept-arte.fr/uk/fiche/atelier_barcelo.html. Consulted 29 February.

MACBA (1998) *Miquel Barceló 1987–1997* [catalogue]. Barcelona: Museo d'Art Contemporani de Barcelona, 3 April–21 June.

Manchado, Trinidad (2000) Cultural Memory, Commerce, and the Arts: The Valencian Institute of Modern Art (IVAM). In Barry Jordan and Rikki Morgan-Tamosunas (eds), *Contemporary Spanish Cultural Studies*, London: Arnold, pp. 92–100.

Manrique, Winston (1999) Las vanguardias históricas dominan el verano. *El País*, 1 July.

Moorman, Margaret (1990) Miquel Barceló. Castelli. *Artnews*, March, p. 178.

Probst Solomon, Barbara (1987) Art in post-Franco Spain. *Artnews*, October, pp. 120–4.

Pulido, Natividad (1999) Cultura busca un espacio anexo al Museo Sorolla para su ampliación. *ABC*, 12 August.

La Razón [anon.] (1999) El nuevo Prado estará acabado en mayo del 2003, un año antes de lo previsto. 18 July.

Reina Sofía (1999) *Miquel Barceló: Obra sobre papel 1979–1999* [catalogue]. Madrid: Museo Nacional Centro de Arte Reina Sofía, 14 September–21 November.

Romero, L. (1999) La ampliación del Museo Thyssen permitirá abrir una sala dedicada a Gauguin. *La Razón*, 4 July.

Rosenbaum, Lee (2000) Brooklyn Hangs Tough. *Art in America*, January, pp. 59, 61, 63, 143.

Sainsbury Centre (1998) *Spain is Different: Post-Pop and the New Image in Spain* [catalogue]. Norwich: Sainsbury Centre for the Visual Arts/ Generalitat Valenciana, July to August.

Samaniego, F. (1999) Jean Nouvel amplía el Museo Reina Sofía con una intervención 'suave y natural'. *El País*, 25 November.

Searle, Adrian (2000) A Relentless Litany of Self-Abuse [review of three British art shows]. *The Guardian* (London), 18 April, section 2, pp. 12–13.

Sierra, Rafael (1999) El Reina Sofía saca a la luz un Barceló íntimo e inédito. *El Mundo*, 15 September.

Smith, Paul Julian (2000) *The Moderns: Time, Space, and Subjectivity in Contemporary Spanish Culture*. Oxford: Oxford University Press.

Spiegel, Olga (1999) El Museu Picasso celebrará su ampliación con una excepcional muestra sobre el artista. *La Vanguardia*, 17 July.

Tío Belido, Ramón (1985) Introduction to *Five Spanish Artists*, 1985: 23–30.

uib (2000) Fons documental Miquel Barceló-Arta; www.uib.es/secc6 biblioteca/secc14/mbarcelo/fons_documental.htm. Consulted 29 February.

Vila-San-Juan, Sergio (1984) *Agenda: Barceló*. Barcelona: Àmbit.

4 Queer Conceptualists? Basque Artists on the Borders

Concepts

It is undoubtedly only with Duchamp that the painters will arrive at a suitable strategy to allow them to use the littérateur without being used in return, and thus to escape the position of structural inferiority in relation to the producers of metadiscourses where they are placed by their status as producers of necessarily mute objects, mute especially about their creators. It is a strategy which consists of denouncing and methodically thwarting – in the conception and the very structure of the work, but also in an anticipated metadiscourse (the obscure and disconcerting title) or in a retrospective commentary – any attempt at annexation of the work by discourse, this being achieved, obviously, without discouraging the exegesis – far from it – that is always so necessary to the fully accomplished social existence of the art object.

(Bourdieu [1992] 1996: 137)

For Arthur C. Danto, conceptual art springs from the aesthetic and institutional consequences of the death of painting in the early 1980s. Formally 'indifferen[t] to the kind of purity [Clement] Greenberg saw as the goal of an historical development', artists and critics who favoured media such as photography also attacked 'the class associations of painting, the institutional implications of the museum of fine arts' (Danto 1997: 137, 138). 'With the philosophical coming of age of art', writes Danto, 'visuality drops away.' It is a disappearance of the object marked in the New York art world by such milestones as when the Guggenheim's director Thomas Krens 'deaccessioned' a Kandinsky and a Chagall in order to acquire a mainly conceptual collection 'much of which did not exist as objects' (16). Ironically, however, this proclamation of the death of painting coincided with 'the tremendous upsurge of painting in the early 1980s', a trend less welcome to art historians than to an art market 'calibrated to the large amounts of disposable capital that fell into [the] hands' of the Reagan era (139).

If we look at one prolific commentator on conceptual art, we see that such problems of chronology are endemic in the definition of the field. Robert C. Morgan cites, successively, as origins for the movement Sol LeWitt's 'Paragraphs on Conceptual Art', published in *Artforum* in 1967 (Morgan 1994: 117); the 'late 1970s' anti-Formalist challenge to the Greenbergian 'institutional avant-garde' of Abstract Expressionism (Morgan 1996: 3); Pop Art's 'abandonment to the media and the marketplace' in 1962 (1996: 4); the 'huge' *Information* show at MOMA in 1970 (1996: 6); and privileged precursor Duchamp, for whom 'art was less a matter of "retinal" pleasure than a provocation that would incite new ideas' (1996: 5). Furthermore, while conceptual art of the 1960s is 'austere and reductive in means of presentation' (exemplified by On Kawar's *Date Paintings*), later neo-conceptualism incorporates more ostentatious references to mass marketing (such as Jenny Holzer's LED *Truisms*) (1996: 14). Since 'each work of conceptual art is different', writes Morgan, 'it would be presumptuous to attempt to write a history' of such a problematic field (1994: pp. xv, 115).

Temporally discontinuous, Morgan's surveys are also typologically ambiguous. Thus he proposes multiple, competing classifications. On the one hand, conceptual art may be defined by its ambitious content: its reach 'beyond formalism', its aim to 'represent content', and its concern for 'politics and ideology'. On the other, it responds (in the USA at least) to three formal methodologies, structural, systemic and philosophical (1996: 7). Treating the absence of the signified, the playing out of a serialized set of components, or exploiting language as its material, conceptual art can also be categorized according to the various media it exploits: documents, photographs and performance. The document serves to 'eliminate the division' between 'the function of the critic and the function of the artist' (1994: 31); the photograph, no longer 'containing the subject' as in fine art practice, serves (as in Victor Burgin's 'photo paths') to 'document an actual site – usually a billboard in an urban setting – which is fed back to the viewer as a recontextualized narrative' (1994: 51, 73); finally, performance renders 'the line between happening and daily life . . . as fluid and indistinct as possible' (1994:

80). If the central problem is to 'make a work of art that has no physical substance' (1994: p. ix), then this 'dropping away' of the visuality of the object is often matched by a fading of the subject: 'the disappearance of the individual as focus of beliefs' (1996: 40). Hence such varied abdications of form, origin and physical presence as Bernar Venet's *Charcoal Sculpture without Specific Shape* (1963), Sherrie Levine's reproductions of pre-existing photographs (early 1980s), and Richard Long's records of a fragile intervention in the landscape (*A Line in Scotland*, 1981) (1996: 111, 129, 177). The ephemeral traces of such works are often reliant on secondary source material (not to mention critical commentary) for the full realization of meaning.

Morgan's general study of conceptual art (1996) overlaps to a large extent with his volume explicitly devoted to 'an American perspective' (1994). But he does gesture toward an acknowledgement of the particularity of artistic reception, even of the most austere and abstract works. Thus Morgan comments on Muntadas, a Spanish artist who has 'since the mid seventies dealt primarily with the process of demystification and deconstruction [of] art and media culture'. In its response to *Exhibition* (1987), a sequence of reverently darkened galleries containing nothing but empty frames, the New York art world failed to notice Muntadas's formal reference to the reliquary, a typology familiar in Spain, preferring to read the work in terms of the US tradition of minimalism (1996: 138, 139, 144). Perilously placed on the border between subject and object, visibility and invisibility, the aesthetic and the everyday, conceptual art can also, however, address and exploit national and cultural differences.

Borders

Because of the nature and extent of day-to-day repression, the Moscow underground was a natural environment for avant-garde conceptual art – that art which in the West evolved out of a broadly shared sense that the object and intention of artists' work needed to be continued free from art-historical or ideological presumptions. The basic philosophical problem of living in a culture where you could not refer to things and experiences by their real names, and in which fully contradictory experiences are the schizogenic way of life, created a condition for the emergence of a conceptual art that varied somewhat from its more academic sources in the West.

(Ross 1990: 22)

One striking, and moving, example of the specificity of conceptual art to its temporal and spatial context is David A. Ross's catalogue *Between Spring and Summer: Soviet Conceptual Art in the Era of Late Communism*. Claiming that the artists included embody 'challenges to art not only in late communist but [also] in late capitalist societies', Ross notes the 'underlying theme of the exhibition': 'the living-death of a particularly dysfunctional modern culture stripped of its soul by decades of cultural engineering' (1990: 3). Ross stresses the borderline quality of the US underground, described as 'a sort of off-Broadway art world where ideas could be readied for the marketplace free from critical tampering, while simultaneously developing the saleable American veneer of absolute independence' (5). 'American radical art', Ross continues, 'has often oscillated between prescribing progressive social change . . . and demand[ing] space for pure aesthetic invention linked to formal issues'. There is thus a 'splintering' between the latter, conceptual art, concerned with 'a philosophical exploration of art, its purpose and its ontological capacities' and the former, political practice that 'directly invokes social issues' (5). While the 'super-utilitarians' are blamed for the demise of 'pure art' (25), in practice progressives and formalists participate in the same omnivorous US art market.

In the end game of the Soviet Union, meanwhile, shared formal or typological properties bear within them different cultural charges. The 'anti-aestheticism' of the Russians, their 'angry hermeticism', derives from a peculiarly Soviet 'refusal to recognize the reductive language of modernism as heroic' (13), and their 'transgressive, Koonsian spirit' (21) from a context in which state propaganda, not consumerism, is the dominant force. The appeal to documents, photographs and ephemeral performance responds to a degree of material privation and political repression inconceivable to US artists who employ similar strategies. Ilya Kabakov's 'monumental' installation *The Man who Flew into Space from his Apartment* (1981–8), a meticulously reproduced domestic setting with a great, jagged hole in the ceiling, is thus informed by a particular pathos, quite different from Western conceptualists' more generalized appeal to the waning of the subject.

However, even before the fall of the Soviet Union, art becomes a staging post on the border between East and West: 1988 sees the first Sotheby's Soviet auction (7); and by 1989 Moscow is awash with Western consumer goods (8). New conditions prompt Ross to ask new questions, centring on the problematic of nationality:

Must an avant-garde function as an oppositional force? what is the
relationship of an art market to the dissolution of a community? will
the Soviet scene generate its own critical press? is the diverse identity
crisis – between region and nation – reflected in art from Moscow? is
the presence of an avant-garde a product of cosmopolitan thinking?

(Ross 1990: 9)

These questions are explored by Peter Wollen in his essay on the
best-known artists in the exhibition, Komar and Melamid. Wollen
argues for the seriousness of the duo's 'art of contradiction, juxtaposition, and irony' (1990). The use of anachronism in this context,
superficially similar to Western postmodernism, relates rather to
Stalin's paradoxical project: 'to combine a Fordist industrial revolution in the base with a neo-tsarist cultural counter-revolution in the
superstructure . . . accelerating towards the future, while reversing
towards the past' (108). While pop art in the West derived from an
encounter with consumerism ('a recognition that the barrier erected
between "high" and "low" art could no longer be maintained'),
Wollen writes that 'it was precisely the failure to deliver consumer
goods that led to the crisis of the Soviet state' (109–110). Exiled to
the USA in the 1970s, Komar and Melamid used pastiche and
parody (most particularly in relation to the Socialist Realism they
repeated and reversed), only to be absorbed into New York's 'flux
of temporal values' in which the new is simply 'what comes later'
(115). What Wollen calls 'the historical nature of the duo's project',
an ambition continued with ironic paintings of the New York
Guggenheim in ruins or heroic photographs of rust belt New Jersey,
was invisible 'through the remorselessly frivolous spectacles of the
Manhattan art world' (115).

Ross writes in his introduction: 'To those who have never directly
experienced a shooting war or real revolution, the ironic use of the
term "underground" implied a desire to consider art as a radical
form of pro-social para-military activity . . . To those who have, the
terms had an altogether different set of connotations' (1990: 23).
But one comparably critical context closer to home for the US art
world, and one in which the death of art was also no metaphor, was
the AIDS epidemic in the Eighties and Nineties. And one rigorously
conceptual artist who actively intervened in this charged political
context was Félix González-Torres, who was consecrated with a
solo show at the New York Guggenheim in Spring 1995 (Spector
1995). In his preface to the catalogue Thomas Krens stresses the
way in which González-Torres transcends the splintering which Ross

saw in the US avant-garde, claiming that González-Torres is 'both aesthetically refined and socially provocative . . . [neither] abstract and contemplative [nor] aggressively political' (Spector 1995: p. viii). Krens comments that González-Torres's 'subdued' voice lightly alludes to such issues as 'the erasure of history, the efficacy of our political system, the bias inherent to gender difference, the pervasiveness of ideology, and the severity of the AIDS crisis'. And Krens stresses both the institutional and the site-specific nature of the exhibition: the Guggenheim, founded to collect and display existing contemporary art, also exhibits 'young artists while their careers are unfolding'; and the installation in Frank Lloyd Wright's rotunda is supplemented by a public project of billboards displaying an enigmatic photograph by González-Torres in sites across the city (Spector 1995: p. ix).

Curator Nancy Spector places González-Torres's practice within the context of the New York art world since the late 1980s, when artists' awareness of the 'exhaustion of the Modernist paradigm [of] authenticity, originality, and rigorous composition' was curiously combined with 'market-driven sensibilities generat[ing] an economic frenzy in the galleries, museums, auction houses' (3). Feminist critique of masterful humanism (from artists such as Jenny Holzer, Sherrie Levine and Cindy Sherman) led to an interest in 'the discourse of others' (4–5), and was the foundation for González-Torres's 'intellectual and conceptually based artistic practice' (10). Dissolving the border between aesthetics and politics (claiming that 'the politics which permeate [aesthetics] are totally invisible' (13)), González-Torres's own 'discourse of the other' shifts subtly between 'cultural activism' and 'personal disclosure', 'ero[ding] the boundaries between [them]' (14). As Spector writes, 'often abstract and almost always untitled, his pieces quietly but persistently bespeak the pleasures and fulfilment of homoerotic desire and same-sex love' (15).

Just as Soviet postmodernism reframed Western conceptual practices, so González-Torres, an openly gay Cuban exile, reappropriated pre-existing forms. His stacks of give-away paper prints mirror minimalist sculpture; his laconic textual pieces echo conceptual date paintings; and his inexhaustible candy spills cite the non-specific shapes of earlier sculptors (16). Non-referential forms are thus subtly infused with content, often homoerotic (17), and the 'cultural barriers between art and social/political context . . . – inside and outside – [are rendered] permeable' (22). For example, the 1986 Supreme Court ruling that 'gay men and lesbians have no protection from government interference, even in the "privacy" of their bedrooms' (23) is obliquely connected to the artist's 1992 billboard project: 'a black and white photograph of an empty, but recently shared double bed, its pillows nestled together and still bearing the fresh indentations of two heads' (25). Refusing the label 'gay artist', González-Torres nevertheless homosexualizes the fall of visuality and loss of the subject typical of the conceptualist's ready-made: two identical clocks tick side by side, the image of 'perfect lovers'; two light bulbs glow intertwined, a vision of queer radiance and evanescence (73). The candy spills, piled in the corners of galleries and offered to the public, also engage more literally in homoerotic desire and despair: for Spector, they are 'parts of one "body" entering the willing mouths of other bodies' (150); for González-Torres, they 'say, simply, "take me"' (156). Yet more seriously, traces on graph paper, apparently minimalist in style, actually chart the T-cell count of González-Torres's ailing lover Ross (167); and fragile light strings cite childhood street parties in Cuba (192). What Spector calls González-Torres's 'softening of the boundaries between the public and private spheres' (192) thus fuses queer politics with conceptualist aesthetics in a uniquely resonant, austere and unstable form. It is a practice, however, that is fully realized only when supplemented by secondary source material and sympathetic critical commentary.

Spaniards-Basques: two territories

> If a self-referential discourse and an autonomous speech arise from the very conditions of possibility which authorize the articulation of 'repressive' frames (whether moral, juridical, or scientific) they do not consequently play the same role in the regime of sexuality. Moreover, as soon as they constitute themselves publicly, lesbian and gay discourses question the criteria of exclusion from that regime . . . although they always, in one way or another, confirm it as a regulatory system, inevitably maintaining some of its exclusionary effects.
>
> (Llamas 1998: 12)

Curiously, perhaps, departments of fine arts in Spanish universities, not known for their progressive inclinations, proved in the 1990s to be among the few foci for the theorization of homosexuality in the public sphere and in the first person.[1] Confirming Bourdieu's hypothesis of the mutual implication of artist and scholar in the accomplishment of the 'social existence of the art object', rare gay-identified scholars, such as Juan Vicente Aliaga, encouraged and documented the 'invasion' of 'a new queer culture'[2] in the Spanish state, a shift which occurred despite the lack of translations of theoretical texts and exhibitions of relevant art works (Aliaga 1999). Moreover, there was also a significant cross-over between conceptual art and queer theory: José Luis Brea, academic commentator on some of the most austere contemporary art, devoted an issue of his magazine *Acción Paralela* to the new trend; Aliaga himself had previously edited a collection on conceptual art, which included essays by US commentator Robert C. Morgan.

Aliaga's 1997 volume of essays *Bajo vientre* (subtitled 'Representations of sexuality in contemporary art and culture') stages multiple and perilous border crossings. The first of these is institutional. In a country in which any personal investment in academic research (whether feminist or gay) is regularly decried as 'subjectivist' or 'reductionist', Aliaga writes as both a university professor and an unashamed militant: the Director General of Museums and Fine Arts in Valencia praises his book for revealing 'a look which knows it is gay and is proud to be so' (Aliaga 1997: 9). And in his introduction, Aliaga, a contributor to the fashionable *Artforum*, rails against the nepotism, formalism and idealism of Spanish art criticism, limits breached by his own intellectual and personal experience of Paris, London and New York (13–14). As in Ross's Soviet Union, then, the critical and artistic avant-garde (in this case, queer) remains politically oppositional and culturally cosmopolitan in a state which still experiences its position as marginal to the global art world.

Elsewhere Aliaga's critical essays, like González-Torres's art works, dissolve the border between politics and aesthetics. A discussion of the links between US feminism and queer theory is illustrated by Man Ray's photographs of enigmatic ready-mades (e.g. the egg whisk titled *Man* (1918)) (23). A denunciation of the homophobic witch hunt of the 'Arny case' (in which closeted celebrities were accused of corrupting minors in a gay Seville pub) is read as a paradigm of the theoretical problem of invisibility and the permeable 'barrier' between public and private spheres (44). Gay and lesbian images from the USA (Robert Mapplethorpe's photographs of embracing black and white youths or fistfuckers, Nicole Eisenman's pornographic cartoons) are juxtaposed with their Spanish opposite numbers (Alex Francés's 'headfucking' photograph; collective LSD's split-crotch 'lesbian sculpture') (69, 75, 81, 87). Essays charting the incorporation of theorists Judith Butler and Deleuze-Guattari into *Artforum* magazine and New York galleries are contrasted with a study of Andalusian conceptualist sculptor, AIDS artist, and disciple of Lacan, Pepe Espaliú.[3] From a relatively protected institutional position (albeit marginalized within his chosen discipline), Aliaga thus provides the exegesis which, as Bourdieu argues once more, is both necessary for the social existence of the art object and particularly resisted by the obscure, disconcerting and mute products of a predominantly conceptual practice. The loss of visuality implicit in much of this art work is thus placed in unstable combination with Aliaga's explicit call to visibility for Spanish lesbians and gays. It is a paradox familiar to the now expert Spanish commentators on, and exegetes of, North American queer theory, such as Ricardo Llamas (1998).

I return a little later to two pioneering exhibitions of contemporary queer art held in the Basque Country. But first we must treat the contested frontiers between international, Spanish and Basque art in their contemporary institutional contexts. It is a striking feature of Spanish arts policy that both private and public funds support some of the most experimental domestic practices. The Fundación Telefónica, Spain's powerful telecommunications conglomerate, consistently shows challenging conceptual art in the gallery located beneath the great tower of its corporate headquarters on Madrid's Gran Vía: Muntadas's multimedia *Proyectos* ('Projects', 1998), Marcel·lí Antúnez Roca's cyber sculpture *Epifanía* ('Epiphany', 1999), and Francesc Roca's *Circuitos cerrados* ('Closed Circuits', 2000), poignant photographs of a ruined motor race-track. Such enigmatic statements on the relation between art and technology recur in group shows held in Spain and abroad. *El punto ciego* ('Blind Spot: Spanish Art of the 90s'), whose best-known artist is Basque constructivist Txomin Badiola, was curated by José Luis Brea and shown at the Kunstraum Innsbruck in 1999. The exhibition was praised by the Austrian administrator for its 'use of an international formal language ... [which shows] younger generations' ... familiarity with digital, virtual audio and video worlds' (Thoman-Oberhofer 1999). In the same year some twenty artists, including Badiola once more, participated in *Existencias Agotadas* ('Exhausted Existences'), an exhibition of electronic art (CD roms and installations) held in the rehabilitated Fuencarral Market in the old centre of Madrid and aiming to 'break down the borders' between artist and public (Dyaz 1999).

The inclusion of Basque (and Catalan) artists in such high-profile events (Innsbruck was supported by the Spanish government, Fuencarral by Apple) is problematized by the curatorial policy of Basque institutions themselves. One telling example is the Fine Arts Museum in Vitoria-Gasteiz, the capital of both the province of Alava and the *autonomía* of Euskalherria. Founded in 1941 as the site for public collections of fine arts, arms and archeology, the now dedicated art museum remains in the Renaissance revival mansion built for the Count of Dávila in 1912 (Museos de Araba 1996). Acquisitions policy was initially dedicated to classical art and Basque 'costumbrismo'. With the death of Franco in 1975, policy shifted to contemporary Spanish art, and since 1985 the Basque government has deposited in the museum the prize-winners of Gure Artea, the annual competition of contemporary Basque art. Spanish classics (e.g. Ribera) and *costumbristas* (e.g. Sorolla), officially described as 'foreign', were thus joined by the third strand of the collection: contemporary art which, because of the museum's avowed 'territoriality', gives priority to work from Alava and the Basque Country, including artists of the 1990s such as Badiola and Cristina Iglesias.

While the Vitoria Museum presents its curatorial policy as an organic development in spite of sixty traumatic years of national history, one more recent and spectacular institution cannot hide its institutional and territorial conflicts: the Bilbao Guggenheim. As is well known, the Guggenheim, funded by local government but with its collection on loan from the New York foundation headquarters, was both attacked as an example of the seductions of cultural imperialism (Zulaika 1997) and celebrated for its role in renovating a depressed urban fabric, previously known for deindustrialization and terrorist violence. In 1998, one year after its opening, a local paper claimed that the museum was 'the pride of all', and that its collection combined North Americans Andy Warhol and Robert Rauschenberg with Basques Txomin Badiola and Eduardo Chillida (Iglesias 1998). Currently the location for glamorous fashion shoots and video clips, Bilbao bears no relation to itself in the 1940s, described by a local writer as 'a city of iron, always wet, shiny, and black because it never stopped raining . . . its streets and houses filthy from chimney smoke . . . a fine imitation of Coketown, the industrial city described by Dickens in *Hard Times*'. Now, by contrast, it is 'white and luminous'.

National commentators describe the continuing controversy over the presence of Basque artists in the Bilbao museum (Villacorta 2000). The core of the collection was the monumental masters of Abstract Expressionism (Rothko, de Kooning and Clifford Still). But an attempt at 'balance between the two extremes of the US and Europe' led to the purchase of fourteen works by German neo-Expressionist painter Anselm Kiefer, intended to echo the role of the key Kandinsky collection in the New York Guggenheim. Before the fears that a museum subsidized from the public purse would have no 'autonomous collection', but would merely be an 'appendix' to the US metropolitan centre, it was agreed that local art would be bought: but only that produced after 1980, when 'Basque society had experienced the changes due to self-rule (*el fenómeno autonómico*)'. Recent purchases included, once more, the young Txomin Badiola. But negotiations proved lengthy and fraught with the elder statesman of Basque sculpture, Chillida. While site-specific commissions were long in place from Italian transvanguardist Francesco Clemente and US feminist conceptualist Jenny Holzer, the location of Chillida's monumental pieces remained undecided (Esteban 2000). Oteiza, the other patriarch of Basque sculpture, had not yet even opened discussions.

Spring 2000 did see, however, a group show at the Guggenheim dedicated to young Basque conceptualists: *La torre herida por el rayo: lo imposible como meta* ('The Tower Struck by Lightning: The Impossible as a Goal'). The prominently displayed and extensive exhibition was intended, according to curator Javier González de Durana, to 'treat the limits of the human being and the struggle s/he maintains to break them, cross them, and attain the physical and intellectual possession of the territory situated beyond those limits' (González de Durana 2000). This existential and aesthetic rupture is expressed in varied works and media all produced in 1999 or 2000. Gabriel Díaz's *El meteorito que cayó en mi casa* ('The Meteorite that Fell on My House') is a video installation digitally imaging a comet as it falls endlessly through space; Javier Pérez's sculpture *La torre de sonido* ('The Tower of Sound') is a great cage of iron shelves holding innumerable blown-glass vessels which murmur when spectators venture inside; Francisco Ruiz de Infante's installation *Puzzle* projects a shadowy figure against ominous photographic collages of a ruined house, its roof half blown away; and finally Mabi Revuelta's sculpture *Rizos de Medusa* ('Medusa's Curls') is a great carpet of black ostrich feathers juxtaposed with the fearsome claws of some mythical creature.

Formally disparate, the works engage in familiar conceptual style with the border between subject and object (the whispering glass vessels), visibility and invisibility (the spectral figure outside the ruined building), and the aesthetic and everyday (the claws and the carpet). But, like the late Soviet avant-garde, the Basque boundary-breakers appeal to an angry hermeticism that is problematically related to their experience of a long-term shooting war that is no mere allegory of para-military underground art. The potential violence implicit in all these pieces (as in the meteorite that hovers always above the house) thus suggests no less resonantly or ambiguously than Kabakov's shattered domestic installation that conceptual art's quest to transcend limits can, in certain circumstances, be as political and social as it is aesthetic or theoretical.

San Sebastián-Bilbao: two exhibitions

> Everything seems to suggest that discussion of what it means to be human; of the powers, pleasures, and perils that the body holds for subjects; of the impact of new technologies on human beings, is reaching such a level of visibility in Western art at the end of the twentieth century that it is difficult to interpret this state of affairs as mere chance.
>
> (Méndez 1999: unnumbered)

The Koldo Mitxelena Kulturunea, named for the Basque grammarian who formalized the language, occupies a prominent position in the centre of San Sebastián-Donostia. Funded by the local government of Gipuzkoa, it contains an exhibition hall, a library and a multi-use space, all dedicated to 'cultural promotion and diffusion' (gipuzkoa 1999). While the centre shows three kinds of exhibitions (originating in other institutions, devised in-house, and commissioned directly from artists), it also has three aims (the subsidy of cultural activities such as shows and competitions, the organization of events such as the annual festival of contemporary dance, and the rehabilitation of spaces for cultural events). In a culturally conservative city, the Koldo Mitxelena stresses its cosmopolitanism and modernity: at the time of writing the only art work shown on its website is a slate circle by Briton Richard Long, the now ubiquitous pioneer of land art also chosen for its website by Barcelona's Caixa art foundation.

Under the direction of co-ordinator Ana Salaverría,[4] the gallery has also followed a relatively risky curatorial policy, often focusing on issues of race, gender and sexuality in contemporary and conceptual art: group shows such as *Orientalismos* (1998) featured the African and Indian paintings of Miquel Barceló and Francesco Clemente and the more sober video works of Bill Viola; *Transgeric@s* (1999, curated by Juan Vicente Aliaga) showcased little known lesbian and gay artists of the Spanish state such as LSD and Alex Francés; a solo show was also devoted to Soledad Sevilla's monumental installation-painting (2000).

El rostro velado: travestismo e identidad en el arte ('The Veiled Face: Transvestism and Identity in Art', 12 June–6 September 1997), curated by José Miguel G. Cortés, Aliaga's colleague at the Valencian Polytechnic University, helped to establish this policy. A large show of some eighteen photographers (only one of whom, Juan Hidalgo, is Spanish), *El rostro* stages multiple border crossings that implicate conceptual practices in time and space. Thus for some artists photography is used, through historical allusion, as a parody of that fine art practice that 'contained' the subject: Joël Peter Witkin's scratchy silver gelatine prints of androgynes and fetuses and Pierre et Gilles's glossy glamour shots of masquerading celebrities. But the chronology of the exhibition is skewed, temporally discontinuous. Man Ray's self-portraits are juxtaposed with those of Warhol, formally similar; lesbian role-player Claude Cahun precedes and perhaps surpasses Cindy Sherman's uncannily similar, if more celebrated, self-disguises. The exhibition thus reveals a secret history of gender dissidence, most particularly amongst European artists little known to the English-speaking art world. Anxious, like the Guggenheim, to represent the two extremes of the West, Cortés focuses both in his choice of artists and in his explication of gender theory on France: Pierre et Gilles and Cahun are joined by an extensive selection of fetishistic performances by arch-onanist Pierre Molinier.

As Ross predicted of the late Soviet art scene, the avant-garde is here the product of cosmopolitan thinking. But cosmopolitanism will have a particular charge in the Basque Country, a stateless nation which straddles the borders of France and Spain. Judith Butler's account of compulsory heterosexuality, perfectly familiar in the Anglo-American academy and gallery, takes on a different perspective when (as here) translated into Basque and stencilled onto the museum's wall. Moreover, the exhibition itself, which in spite of some graphic sexual material incited no protests from respectable *donostiarras*, was supplemented by lectures in the centre given by external academics, such as Aliaga and myself (sponsored by the British Council). While Cortés's catalogue essay gives an overview of 'the social construction of sex and gender' that interested students would be hard pressed to find in a Spanish university, Gipuzkoa's Delegate of Culture and Basque [language] praises the exhibition for confirming Baudrillard's dictum that 'We are all symbolic transvestites' (Cortés 1997: 310, 297). In the particular cultural and intellectual field of the Spanish state, then, the public-sponsored art gallery becomes a unique space for discussion of queer theory habitually excluded from the university.

But Ricardo Llamas, one of the most sophisticated commentators on this conundrum, warns us that such self-referential discourse and autonomous speech will tend to preserve some of the exclusionary effects of the realm of sexuality in which they are produced. And it could be argued that these multiple discursive frames (North American theory, European cultural institution, and lavishly produced polyglot catalogue) serve rather to contain (or in Bourdieu's word 'annex') the visual works which they claim modestly to serve. It remains the case, however, that in a city haunted by political violence (the assassination by ETA of local politician Miguel Angel Blanco would soon send shock waves through San Sebastián), *El rostro velado* offered an example, marginal and eccentric as it was, of collaboration across cultural and sexual borders.

The unique potential of queer alliances to go beyond social limits was also shown by an exhibition held in a very different setting: *Trans Sexual Express* at Bilbao Arte (8 January–6 February 1999). A modestly proportioned, albeit recently renovated, cultural centre subsidized by the city council and discreetly sited in the old town, Bilbao Arte could not be further from the dazzling titanium Guggenheim. And the exhibition, curated by Xavier Arakistain,[5] a doctoral candidate at the University of the Basque Country, featured twenty young Basque artists, many of whom were completely unknown (Arakistain 1999). Yet, in spite of the territoriality of the selection (with 'Basque' defined loosely as anyone born or active in Euskadi), the works display an international formal language familiar from the beginnings of conceptual art: structural, systemic and philosophical. Txomin Badiola's *Nobody's City* (large-format colour photographs of androgynes suspended over anonymous urban backgrounds) stages the loss of the referent; Manu Arregi's *Yonny de Winter* (a multi-exposed image of a queen dancing and posing) explores seriality; and Lucia Onzain's video *Puta* ('Whore') takes the language of sexual insult as artistic matter.

These formal methodologies are combined, as in *El rostro velado*, with temporal and spatial hiatuses. Despite the contemporaneity of these young artists, they still invoke and rearticulate the past: Ignacio Goitia (*En los jardines de Chantilly* ('In Chantilly Gardens')) parodies Matisse's circle of dancers by transforming them into muscular male nudes; Santi Saiz (*The Man without Shame*) dons Warhol's white wig for a self-portrait; and Miguel Angel Gaüeca (*Intentando enfocar los pies de la mujer ideal* ('Trying to Focus on the Ideal Woman's Feet')) repopulates a typically suburban kitchen with a couple of men dressed only in carnival masks, transparent plastic aprons and high-heeled mules. Such exercises in contradiction, juxtaposition and irony seem initially as frivolous as any in novelty-obsessed New York. But in Bilbao, once more, the effect and implications are different. For Francoist Spain, like Stalinist Russia, had experienced a contradictory chronology in which (in the Basque Country above all) rapid industrial acceleration was combined with equally fierce political repression and cultural reversal. Artists too young to remember the regime still register the effects of a relatively late encounter with consumerism which renders the formal method of pop politically engaged.

Such discrete and enigmatic social critique is confirmed (as in San Sebastián) by the discursive frames which render the work visible and legible. Thus Arakistain proudly calls attention to the equal participation of women and men in the exhibition; and the catalogue is graced by an essay by Lourdes Méndez, a practitioner of the feminist philosophy still rare in the Spanish university system. The personal and intellectual debt of gay men and queer theory to women and feminism is thus acknowledged and celebrated. And as in San Sebastián, once more a series of well-attended lectures by visiting academics also explored these two linked but under-represented fields. Arguably, then, the art scene of rust belt Bilbao, a city still plagued by social problems, was stimulated as much by this modest and local exploration of borders in Bilbao Arte as by the spectacular international interventions of the Guggenheim.

Txomin Badiola: the game of the other

> The Badiola of the conceptual and minimalist sculptures gives way, in this exhibition, to the more literary Badiola, with new languages, new demands on the viewer. We find ourselves before eight installation-narratives which treat concerns that worry not just Badiola: politics, violence, sex, everyday life, culture . . . The mise en scènes devised by the artist, the characters who people them, the objects which compose them, play with the viewer, inviting him or her to enter the spaces thus created, to approach the objects, look through their holes, and take part, surpassing the role of subject of perception, becoming the subject of participation.
>
> (Koruko Aizarna, in Badiola 1997: 5)

Txomin Badiola is perhaps the emblematic post-Franco Basque artist, condensing as he does in his career the conceptual, national and sexual contradictions characteristic of his time and place. A typical Basque border-crosser, Badiola, born in 1957, lived and worked briefly in London and then for seven years in New York, before returning to his native Bilbao in 1998. After showing in the 1980s in local galleries and museums and winning the Basque Sculpture Prize, in the 1990s Badiola made the leap to prestigious exhibition spaces, national and international, public and private, and was proclaimed an 'artist for the twenty-first century' by national daily

El Mundo (Jiménez 2000). Thus he is represented in Madrid by Soledad Lorenzo, as are celebrity Spanish painters Miquel Barceló and Guillermo Pérez Villalta and young British video artists Sam Taylor-Wood and Jane and Louise Wilson (Lorenzo 1998); and he represented Spain in group shows from the Seville Expo 1992 to the Hanover Expo 2000, via the Innsbruck 'Spanish Art of the 90s', curated by José Luis Brea. Fascinated by technology, Badiola took part in the experimental electronic art show in Fuencarral, Madrid (1999), while his work is collected by the most prestigious Basque and, even, Catalan foundations: the Vitoria Fine Arts Museum, the Bilbao Guggenheim, and the Barcelona MACBA and Caixa collections. Badiola was granted a large solo show at the Koldo Mitxelena in San Sebastián in 1997 and lent his prestige to the group *Trans Sexual Express* in Bilbao Arte in 1999.

In spite of this now consecrated career, Badiola's work is diverse, and his artistic trajectory discontinuous. The piece chosen for the 1992 Expo catalogue is an austere conceptual sculpture: a wooden box structure, mimicking a desk, bolted half-way up the gallery wall and furnished with a chair fixed within it in such a way as to render sitting impossible (*Pasajes* 1992: 45). The text accompanying this piece in the catalogue stresses Badiola's Basque filiation: his 'minimalist' and 'constructivist' languages derive from the patriarch of Basque theoretical sculpture, Oteiza, with whom Badiola had 'an intense relationship' (44). Likewise, the introductory essay to the catalogue stresses both Badiola's discovery of 'the up-to-date philosophy of discontinuity and *difference*' and 'his need to define an ethical space for art as the bequest of Basque culture' (28). This is a 'social discourse', engaging a 'critical transformation of [the] experience of life'. The mute conceptual object is here endowed by the scholar with an exegesis that inserts it into both art history and critical theory, thus facilitating its social existence.

We shall look later at the annexation of Badiola's enigmatic works by the discourse of both critic and artist. But first comes the description of his solo show in San Sebastián, *Bestearen jokoa/El juego del otro* ('The Game of the Other', 21 March–24 May 1997). The exhibition is composed of eight installations, gifted with enigmatic titles and boasting a wealth of mixed media. *Recuerda: la gente podría decir si estás sonriendo al otro lado de la línea* ('Remember: People Could Tell if you are Smiling on the Other Side of the Line') is most reminiscent of Badiola's early Basque minimalist manner: six laminated wooden screens (reminiscent of open-plan offices) are set at angles and interspersed with six chairs, whose back-rests are stamped with holes. A thick white rope snakes through the holes and around the

10 Txomin Badiola, *Ordinary Life (with Two Characters Pretending to be Human)* (1995–6), video still. Courtesy of the artist.

screens. *Será mejor que cambies (para mejor)* ('You Better Change (for the Better)') shows the new New York manner: two video projections and large-format photographs show a couple of young androgynes in matching Afro wigs, Y-fronts, and pink and yellow plastic tops. The figures flick through magazines, paint their toe nails, and attempt to strangle one another, as garbled voices vociferate on the soundtrack. Meanwhile, a sauna-like wood construction displays posters of Bruce Lee and Chow Yun Fat. *Ciudad de nadie* ('Nobody's City'), also shown at Bilbao Arte, is seven photos of sexually indifferent figures, silver hair and frosted lips, suspended open-mouthed above a blurry urban landscape. *Vida cotidiana (con dos personajes pretendiendo ser humanos)* ('Ordinary Life (with Two Characters Pretending to be Human')) features three photos of a muscular black and white male couple, wearing only camouflage masks and shorts, slow dancing, while a five-minute video has them play with a pistol to the instrumental track of Herman's Hermits 'How do you do (what you do to me)?'

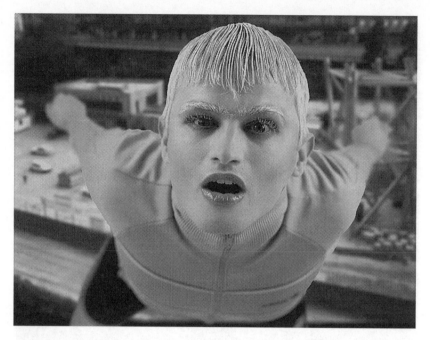

11 Txomin Badiola, *Nobody's City* (1996), photograph. Courtesy of the artist.

12 Txomin Badiola, *You Better Change (for the Better)* (1996), video still.

The title installation, *El juego del otro* ('The Game of the Other'), offers a wooden screen with three apertures through which can be seen a photo of a naked black youth with a club on his shoulder. In *La guerra ha terminado* ('The War is Over') artfully posed Asian youths are photographed in stages of undress, as if in a locker room. But they sit on conceptual sculptures (which are also displayed in the gallery): enigmatic wooden structures (benches? boxes?) linked, once more, by lengths of rope. *El amor es más frío que la muerte* ('Love is Colder than Death') boasts a blow-up of a found photo of a youthful Fassbinder[6] before a table covered with guns and an electric guitar, suspended upside down in the gallery, that endlessly plays the same chord with a mechanically revolving plectrum. Finally, *Tres tipos esperan* ('Three Guys are Waiting') offers the most explicit theoretical reference. A trio of white urban youths, powdered with red, blue and green pigment, sit around a table bearing video equipment and a copy of Deleuze and Guattari's *Anti-Oedipus*. These three photos are supplemented by three plastic seats and speakers emitting an indistinct text, half drowned by electronic music.

The formal language is familiar from international conceptualism, both in its earlier minimalist and its later mass media versions. Structural, systemic and philosophical in turn (engaging with the lost signified, serial repetition and language as material), the exhibition also employs the media favoured by the anti-modernist avant-garde (documents, photography and video records of performance). The subject blurs into the object, the visible fades into invisibility, the aesthetic mutates into the everyday: the wooden structures resist human habitation, the photographic or video figures are absent from the gallery, the detritus of art and life (press clippings and furniture, wigs and guitars) is swept up into heterotopic installations. The fall of visuality, with blurry video images and formless carpentry, thus fuses with the fading of the subject, now simply 'pretending to be human'. Badiola's 'game of the other', then, can be read as the same: a typically New York focus on urban alienation in a global era. Certainly the overt multiculturalism of the show remains unrepresentative of the demographics of the Basque Country.

So far, so cosmopolitan. Yet the out-of-focus urban backdrops to 'Nobody's City' are in fact images of Bilbao. And Badiola's fragmentary narratives can be reread within national and queer frames of legibility. Badiola's persistent melancholia, his stress on a potential violence, frozen but threatening, also read differently in the Basque Country than in the USA, where urban violence lacks such specific political implications. Suspended above the city to which they do not belong, Badiola's androgynes thus allegorize a schizogenic or de-territorialized existence that is both that of the nomadic artist and his spectator, caught between an international hermetic style of production and a very localist context of consumption. The repeated iconographic references to homoeroticism read differently in different national contexts. As we have seen, even González Torres's most abstracted ready-mades (the identical ticking clocks or dented pillows) were produced and received as aesthetic and social comments on the political position of lesbians and gay men in the USA. Badiola's much more explicit photos of muscular black and white youths seem to cite Mapplethorpe, but in the Spanish state they are deprived to a large extent of the interpretative charge provided by the relative visibility of openly queer artists and theorists in the USA. The Badiola who, like the majority of Spanish artists and critics, chooses to make no personal identification of sexual bias is thus poised between abstraction and reference, playfully invoking and disavowing both national and sexual specificity. If Badiola displays, like González Torres, a tension between minimalism and self-disclosure (he himself posed as one of the angels flying above his native city), then the personal references are more hermetic, more angry.

Methodically thwarting critical annexation of his purposefully open-ended works (in part through the traditional strategy of obscure and disconcerting titles), Badiola also uses the *littérateur* without being used in turn. José Luis Brea's catalogue notes, which oscillate between poetic reconstruction and theoretical commentary, at once facilitate and preclude the work's social assimilation. Thus Brea cites explicit analogues from Nietzsche, Benjamin and Deleuze (on the remote possibility of happiness, the decline of experience and the schizoid (1997: 107, 101)), that will enable select spectators to integrate mute or cacophonous art works into a familiar discursive context. But this discourse of the other or of the border ('Who is the other one, which other one am I? Are you on this side, or . . . am I the one who is on the other side?' (102)) is resolutely non-specific. The 'multiculturalism' of young black, white and Asian bodies is dissolved into a plea for 'the West . . . to definitively revise its relationship with discourse' (102); and the erotics of sameness (whether imaged in bodies or chairs) becomes a 'space of representation', of transparency without intimacy (103). The curator-essayist (generally chosen by the artist)[7] thus completes and fulfils the work, granting it a discursive coherence which, ironically, the work itself cannot exhibit if it is to be granted the aesthetic status it demands.

Nobody's territory

The emphasis on communication, on contact [in my work], is not necessarily linked to what is communicated but to the interposition of something which establishes the link. The really important thing is that this
link is not produced between two perfectly defined and closed beings, but
that, in some way, it constitutes them. Communication is produced to
the extent that subjects, in themselves little more than a field of unstable
probabilities, acquire in the communicative act a moment of 'stasis', a
moment in which they are properly configured as such. The work of art
is precisely this catalyst for the Representation to which we all belong and
from which we cannot escape.

(Txomin Badiola, in Lorenzo 1998)

We have seen that conceptual art, difficult indeed to define or delimit,
has as its impossible goal the elimination of the division between
critic and artist in a work that has no physical substance. The problem is that in their habitual abdication of form, origin and physical
presence (often philosophically informed by a critique of transcendence and authority) conceptual artists may in practice collude with
repressive forces that prevent us from referring to things by their
real names. While the positions of Soviet dissidents, Basques and
queers could hardly be more different, as artists they share the same
structural paradox in their relation to a dominant order that they
contest with oblique symbolic forms.

'Autonomous speech', Ricardo Llamas's definition of a queer
discourse at once facilitated and delimited by existing regimes of
visibility, takes on a peculiar charge in a stateless nation such as the
Basque Country, which has achieved self-government only relatively
recently, and whose borders remain unstable. And if it is unlikely
that public subsidy could be given in the USA (as it is in Spain)
without controversy to works of such graphic homoerotic content as
those I have treated here, then it is equally unlikely that US critics
(like their equivalents in Spain once more) would simply fail to
mention that same homoerotic content. The regime of representation to which (according to Badiola) we all belong constitutes some
subjects in different ways from others. Citing the title of Brea's
Innsbruck exhibition, homosexuality thus might be seen as a 'blind
spot' in Spanish culture, just as Spanish art remains a relative absence
in the international art world. However, the aim of queer theory was
of course to destabilize borders between straight and gay, masculine
and feminine; and at least one prominent US artist who explicitly

eroticizes the male body also fails to identify as gay, preferring to aim for a utopian 'sexual indifference'.[8]

I have argued elsewhere (Smith 1996) that this hostility to identity politics is peculiarly strong in Spain. Recently, however, Spanish lesbians and gays, even those who are most theoretically informed, have called quite simply for visibility.[9] The Basque Country in particular boasts the longest-running activist organization in the Spanish state, complete with a publicly funded community centre in the heart of old Bilbao.[10] While the demands of this group are surely unattainable (including as they do the abolition of armies and the full independence of Euskalherria), they take place within a radical militant context that has real effects in the world. More modestly and effectively, Xavier Arakistain's *Trans Sexual Express* (1999) showed the material benefits of collaboration between gay men and women: the exhibition was part funded by Ekamunde, the Basque Women's Institute.

In his work since *El juego del otro* and his return to residence in Bilbao, Badiola himself has become more explicit (albeit typically ironic) in his treatment of Basqueness. *Gimme Shelter* (1999) is an installation consisting of a wooden structure decorated with curtains and neon and housing photographs and two video monitors. Images include an *ertzaina* (Basque policeman) reading a book called *Prehistoric Man in the Basque Country* and a *dantzari* (traditional dancer) engrossed in a *Captain America* comic (Jiménez 2000). The ambitions of both nationalist tradition and globalist domination are thus mordantly satirized. In written texts Badiola has also given his own sarcastic narrative of the transformation of Bilbao. When he returned from New York, a friend asked him how he could hope to 'find in these surroundings a catalogue of signs or images comparable to those offered by a culture like the American, in which by definition everything is Pop, everything is image, from politics and religion to the latest consumer product'. The question, writes Badiola, ignored the changes of the last decade:

> The Bilbao I left ten years ago, the Bilbao of industrial decline and daily battles in the streets, unemployment, depression, blackness, and lack of opportunities has nothing in common with the present postmodern Bilbao of the 'Guggenheim Era'. The laborious, grey Bilbao of the ditch and umbrella has given way to the Bilbao of the society column, where the presentation of a prize to a nonentity in ETB [Basque Television] takes on the pomp and ceremony of the Oscars, but with an accordion and a tambourine; where village women have their opinion of Rauschemberg [*sic*] and children adopt a Jeff Koons's

sculpture as a pet, [it is] the city of the truce where improbable political alliances are condemned to work and where it is rash to ask for
political impossibilities because they may come true; in sum, it is a
city that is little modern in its heart, forced to be the most postmodern
and all this is made possible by the game of signs and gestures in
which appearance (selling an image) is not just more than being, but
the only form of being. In such surroundings you mustn't lament the
scarcity of signs, it's precisely the avalanche of signs that you have to
deal with.

(Lorenzo 1998)

With typically caustic humour, then, Badiola celebrates both the
fusion of art and everyday life in the Guggenheim era and the potential for real social change in a postmodern politics of image and
performance.

The melancholia of the transparent society, from which all intimacy is rigorously excluded, is thus transcended to some extent by a
stress on art's role as a catalyst in communal communication. While
Badiola's practice is based on a broadly deconstructive or psychoanalytic theory in which language or desire precede the speakers or
lovers caught in their web (a theory made concrete in his love of
'incomplete and open images, forms, and spaces' (Lorenzo 1998)),
his stress on the intersubjectivity that precedes all sense of self can
be read positively as an aspiration to new, more flexible forms of
community that incorporate the discourses and games of others. It
is, in the name of a French exhibition in which he participated, a
'transfrontier' (Art Contemporain 1990), nobody's territory. But it
is precisely, and ironically, this discontinuous subject position, also
uncovered by one scholar in recent melancholy and masochistic
Basque fiction (Gabilondo 1998: 119), that offers the possibility of
rewriting hidden histories of national and sexual dissidence within
the context of the international formal idiom that is conceptual art.

Notes

1 A further example of queer theory in the Spanish fine arts academy is
  Xosé M. Buxán 1997, the proceedings of a conference organized by
  Buxán at the University of Vigo in 1995.
2 Aliaga's use of the English word bears witness to 'queer's incorporation
  and examination in Spain, where its fluidity and flexibility are frequently
  stressed. See Mira 1999 (s.v. 'queer') for an informed and balanced
  discussion of the term and its possible resonance in a Spanish context.
3 For a discussion of Espaliú within the context of Spanish representations
  of AIDS, see Smith 1996.

4 My thanks are due to Ms Salaverría for her hospitality and for providing me with materials, including a video and catalogue of Txomin Badiola's exhibition.

5 My thanks are due to Mr Arakistain for his hospitality and for providing me with information concerning the gestation of the exhibition. The proposal for funding stresses the inclusivity of an exhibition which includes women and men, defines 'Basque artist' broadly as all those living and working in Euskadi, and leavens elitist conceptual art with more accessible club culture: disco diva Alaska appeared as DJ at the opening event.

6 Badiola's written texts also cite sources such as Fassbinder, Genet and Montaigne that are problematic in his work, but are often taken outside Spain to be signs of a queer culture. See Lorenzo 1998.

7 In an unpublished paper (1999), Xosé M. Buxán discusses a similar case in which a commentator chosen by an artist fails to mention the explicitly homoerotic content of the work.

8 The artist is Matthew Barney; see Aliaga 1997: 171–91.

9 The first number of *Reverso* (2000), subtitled 'a journal of lesbian, gay, bisexual, transsexual, transgendered . . . studies', calls for an end to the 'silence' on homosexuality in Spanish culture.

10 EHGAM and its magazine *Gay Hotsa* celebrated their twentieth birthday in 1995.

References

Aliaga, Juan Vicente (1997) *Bajo vientre: representaciones de la sexualidad en la cultura y el arte contemporáneos.* Valencia: Generalitat.

—— (1999) Arte *queer* en España. In Mira 1999: 86–7.

Arakistain, Xabier (curator) (1999) *Trans Sexual Express*. Bilbao: Ayuntamiento.

Art Contemporain (1990) Exposition Pello Irazu, Txomin Badiola / 12 juillet 1990–15 septembre 1990 / France, Troyes (10), Passages-Centre d'art contemporain / Transfrontières, sculptures espagnoles, installations, www.art-contemporain.eu.org/base/chronologie/2057.html. Consulted 25 May 2000.

Badiola, Txomin (1997) *Bestearen jokoa/El juego del otro*. San Sebastián: Diputación Foral de Gipuzkoa.

Bourdieu, Pierre ([1992] 1996) *The Rules of Art: Genesis and Structure of the Literary Field.* Cambridge: Polity.

Brea, José Luis (1997) Txomin Badiola: The Return of the Storyteller. In Badiola 1997: 101–7.

Buxán, Xosé (ed.) (1997) *Conciencia de un singular deseo: estudios lesbianos y gays en el estado español.* Barcelona: Laertes.

—— (1999) Roberto González Fernández: ¿un arte homoerótico de raices británicas? Unpublished paper read at 'Gender Identities at the End of the Century', University of Alcalá, 25–7 October.

Cortés, José Miguel G. (curator) (1997) *Irudi lausotua: trabestismoa eta identitatea artean/El rostro velado: travestismo e identidad en el arte*. San Sebastián: Diputación Foral de Gipuzkoa.

Danto, Arthur C. (1997) *After the End of Art: Contemporary Art and the Pale of History*. Princeton: Princeton University Press.

Dyaz, Antonio (1999) Arte en la red: imágenes cibernéticas. *Diario del Navegante*, 1 October. www.el-mundo.es/navegante/diario/99/octubre/01/luna.ciberarte.html. Consulted 24 May 2000.

Esteban, Iñaki (2000) El Guggenheim retoma el diálogo con Chillida para garantizar su presencia en el museo. www.diario-elcorreo.es/guggenheim/archivo/970812cu.htm. Consulted 24 May.

Gabilondo, Joseba (1998) Terrorism as Memory: The Historical Novel and Masculine Masochism in Contemporary Basque Literature. *Arizona Journal of Hispanic Cultural Studies*, 2, pp. 113–46.

gipuzkoa (1999) www.gipuzkoa.net/kultura/km/castellla/01expo.htm. Consulted 23 May 2000.

González de Durana, Javier (2000) La torre herida por el rayo: lo imposible como meta. *@Guggenheim: Guía del Museo Guggenheim Bilbao* (February–June), unpaginated.

Iglesias, Lucía (1998) Bilbao: el efecto Guggenheim. www.elcorreodigital.com/guiaocio/cultura/museosviz.html. Consulted 23 May 2000.

Jiménez, José (2000) Txomin Badiola: insatisfacción. *El Mundo en Internet*, 29 April. www.el-mundo.es/diario/impresora.html?noticia=/2000/04/29/cultura/. Consulted 25 May 2000.

Llamas, Ricardo (1998) *Teoría torcida: prejuicios y discursos en torno a 'la homosexualidad'*. Madrid: Siglo XXI.

Lorenzo, Soledad (1998) Txomin Badiola. www.soledadlorenzo.com/esp/index.html. Consulted 25 May 2000.

Méndez, Lourdes (1999) Trans Sexual Express: recorridos artísticos por cuerpos, géneros, e identidades de sexo. In Arakistain 1999 (unnumbered).

Mira, Alberto (ed.) (1999) *Para entendernos: diccionario de cultura homosexual, gay, y lésbica*. Barcelona: Tempestad.

Morgan, Robert C. (1994) *Conceptual Art: An American Perspective*. Jefferson, NC, and London: McFarland.

—— (1996) *Art into Ideas: Essays on Conceptual Art*. Cambridge and New York: Cambridge University Press.

Museos de Araba (1996) www.arco.ifema.es/gen.htm. Consulted 25 May 2000.

Pasajes: Spanish Art Today (1992) Seville: Electa.

Reverso: Revista de estudios lesbianos, gays, bisexuales, transexuales, transgénero . . . , número uno: La producción del silencio (2000), 1.

Ross, David A. (curator) (ed.) (1990) *Between Spring and Summer: Soviet Conceptual Art in the Era of Late Communism*. Boston: Institute of Contemporary Art.

Smith, Paul Julian (1996) Fatal Strategies: The Representation of AIDS in the Spanish State. In *Vision Machines: Cinema, Literature, and Sexuality in Spain and Cuba, 1983–93*, London and New York: Verso, pp. 101–27.

Spector, Nancy (curator) (1995) *Félix González-Torres*. New York: Guggenheim Museum.

Thoman-Oberhofer, Elisabeth (1999) *El punto ciego*. Spanish Art of the 90's: November 7th–January 23rd 1999. www.kunstraum-innsbruck.at/etext100.htm%preface. Consulted 24 May 2000.

Villacorta, José Luis (2000) La colección: una oferta en fase incipiente. http://google.netscape.com/netscape?query=%22txomin+badiola%22. Consulted 23 May 2000.

Wollen, Peter (1990) Scenes from the Future: Komar and Melamid. In Ross 1990: 107–20.

Zulaika, Joseba (1997) *Crónica de una seducción: El museo Guggenheim Bilbao*. Madrid: Nerea.

5 Catalan Independents? Ventura Pons's Niche Cinema

US independents

> This was a good day . . . We got a green light on a feature motion picture
> . . . We can go for it, secure in the knowledge that we haven't made one
> aesthetic decision as a result of being umbilically attached to a marketing
> department. . . . While in the best of all possible worlds, independent films
> are genuinely alternative, genuinely original visions, there's no such thing
> as an absolutely independent film.
>
> (Vachon 1998: 16)

The artistic industry, or industrial art *par excellence*, film exhibits to
an extreme degree the paradoxes of aesthetic autonomy and social
control explored by Bourdieu's sociology of culture.[1] And nowhere
are those paradoxes so keenly felt as in the much-discussed, but ill-
defined, niche known as 'independent cinema'. One US collection
of interviews with 'independent filmmakers' defines its subject matter
in turn as 'critical', 'avant-garde', 'revolutionary', 'poetic', 'alternative', 'transnational' and 'queer' cinema (MacDonald 1998: 1).

While the directors who feature in this volume are truly institution-
ally marginal, confined overwhelmingly to 8 mm and 16 mm, popular accounts by self-defined 'independent' producers and distributors
focus on 35 mm feature films. Christine Vachon, one of the most
respected of US producers, offers a detailed guide to 'making movies
that matter' over the last decade (1998). Vachon traces a notional
project: from development, through budget, financing and dealing
with actors and crew to the shoot itself, postproduction, and distribution, marketing and release. And she supplements this general

advice with 'diary interludes' tracing the specific production process of two recent features: *I Shot Andy Warhol* and *Velvet Goldmine*. Vachon and her colleagues call attention to a number of shifts in the film business. For example, 'distributors are more in the prebuying business than they used to be' (and thus demand some creative input), while a changing market is 'more theatrically driven' because of the decline of the home video market (Vachon 1998: 124–5). On the one hand, Vachon laments the 'drying up' of state and federal funds in the USA; but on the other, she attacks public-funded European filmmakers who are 'indifferent to their prospective audience' (128–9). Or again, 'casting has come to play an increasing large role in preselling a film' for 'indie dependents' (128, 131), while optioning a book property or foreign pre-sales can also help (133, 135). But government-funded European TV stations are now 'sinking fast', with Britain's Channel 4 one of the few still buying broadcast rights that fund both production costs and theatrical distribution (136).

'Actors', writes Vachon, 'are the single most important element in a film', with 'the financing of even small, independent films becom[ing] more cast-driven' (145, 154). Yet independents can still achieve unexpected success with unlikely projects. Contradicting the received wisdom that 'No one's going to see a gay film in Chinese!', Ang Lee's *The Wedding Banquet* 'earned four thousand per cent on its investment' (239, 299). And 'stay[ing] true to the director's vision', such films can 'lead the audience instead of following its dictates' (272). While pessimistic producers say that distribution is where you 'pay the price for independence' (285), niche marketing can counteract even poor reception at festivals and hostile notices from critics: 'If your movie has something that ties it to a particular community – be it gay, black, Latino, etc. – it has a good chance of finding a place on a well-entrenched circuit' (296).

The most recent changes seem the most disheartening. Sundance, the famous independent festival, has become 'the most commercial film festival on earth [with] discourse about film' swamped by talk about money (297). And 'independents, structurally at least, are the victims of their own success' (313). While ten years earlier a film such as *Howard's End* 'played on particular screens for sixty weeks', now after the first weekend's grosses, distributors have to decide whether to 'throw another million or two million into the pot to see if [the film] will break' (that is, go wide across the country), such is the speed with which films are 'thrown off' screens (314). However, writes Vachon optimistically, once the marginal becomes mainstream, then it too will be replaced: Sundance has spawned the younger, kickier Slamdance (319).

An alternative to Vachon's production-based history is distributor John Pierson's 'guided tour across a decade of independent American cinema', *Spike, Mike, Slackers, & Dykes* (1995). Pierson's more linear narrative is framed by 1984's *Stranger than Paradise* and 1994's *Pulp Fiction*, with Steven Soderbergh's 1989 *sex, lies, and videotape* 'neatly divid[ing] things down the middle' (Pierson 1995: 2). Pierson focuses on the niche markets he helped to fill by contributing to the finance of original productions such as *She's Gotta Have It* (African American) and *Go Fish* (lesbian). But he also gives, incidentally, an account of the complex relationship between US independents and European films.

In the Sixties and Seventies combined, distributors and exhibitors such as Dan Talbot's New Yorker and Pierson's own Jean Renoir specialized in their 'high quality libraries' of Fassbinder, Bresson, Ozu and Herzog (13). Even in the early Eighties a company such as United Artists Classics started by distributing French features such as *Le Dernier Métro*, *Diva* and *Coup de foudre* (17). 'Entering the mid-eighties', however, 'there was one enormous change afoot in the business, which would enhance the prospects for all English-language features while fatally wounding specialized repertory exhibition' (19). This was home video. While 'the specialized theatrical audience didn't seem to differentiate that strongly between American, British, or foreign titles', video distributors strongly favoured the first. The death of repertory thus also signalled the collapse of European market share in the USA. While, most unusually, in 1988 Orion Classics could 'score four times in a row on the foreign language side with Louis Malle's *Au Revoir les enfants*, the Danish *Babette's Feast*, Wim Wenders's . . . *Wings of Desire*, and Pedro Almodóvar's New York Film Festival opener *Women on the Verge of a Nervous Breakdown*' (120), foreign film buffs such as Pierson would play a leading role in promoting a generation of US independents whose movies would take the place of European films on specialized US screens. Moreover, those filmmakers they championed made a virtue of their ignorance of foreign film: Kevin Smith, director of the black-and-white, minimalist narrative *Clerks*, says in conversation with Pierson: 'I'm a student of American independent cinema . . . I don't feel I have to go back and view European or other foreign films because I feel like these guys [i.e. earlier US independents] have already done it for me, and I'm getting filtered through them' (32). While this 'ethic' (his word) may satisfy Smith, things look different from the other side of the Atlantic.

EU independents?

Independence [can] be defined as exclusion, as always being on the outside.

(Corbett 1999: 17)

Angus Finney's *The State of European Cinema* (1996; based initially on a report written for the European Film Academy and *Screen International* in 1993) reconfirms that 'the dwindling foreign-language market in the US has, in part, been taken over by a burgeoning independent sector' (Finney 1996: 13). The figures are clear. 'In 1993 some 250 low budget US indie films were made, compared to about 500 in 1995' (12–13). This 'glut' is fighting for release with foreign films, whose collapse in US market share was astonishingly swift: from a healthy 6.4 per cent in 1986 to 0.75 per cent in 1994 (15). Finney also raises a question that was not posed by Vachon in the USA: the training needs of an industry suffering from increased casualization. In the UK the Independent Production Training Fund was created in 1993 and funded by a levy on production budgets (41). Such measures are, however, 'less prevalent across Europe than might be expected' (41).

Ironically, it is a US indie director, Hal Hartley, who raised the substantial issue at a conference of the European Film Academy in Berlin, asserting that 'aesthetics and economics are intertwined when it comes to film-making' (136). Given the relative failure of European film in both fields, Finney asks some pointed questions:

> When is subsidy given out just for cultural reasons, and what result does that approach have for the mid- to longer-term health of the film industry? Do public funders and committees ask themselves about a film's ability to find a place in the market, or are they too often more concerned with political, social, and employment effects? Which national incentive mechanisms could stimulate a stronger European industry if applied on a wider and longer-term scale? (136)

Surprisingly perhaps, one answer comes from a relatively neglected territory: Spain. The cause of the mid-Nineties 'Spanish upswing' in production and market share is the automatic subsidy scheme introduced in 1995, under which 'the Spanish Film Institute (ICAA) now awards a grant of 33 per cent of a film's budget to any Spanish film that takes more than pta 30 million ($230,000) at the [domestic] box office, up to a maximum value pta 100 million ($773,000) per film' (121). Not only does this encourage producers to make more commercial films; it also means, according to distinguished producer Andrés Vicente Gómez, that 'producers can also start their own films without having to go through committees' (Finney 1996: 121). Ironically, speedier production schedules and the imposition of more commercial criteria helped to promote artistic independence. Previous arrangements for advance subsidy on a project-by-project basis both 'distorted the market' by inflating budgets and encouraged the production of films that 'had little chance of recouping [costs] at the box office' (121).

The trade press reinforces this sense of confusion as to the history and status of 'independent' audiovisual production in Europe.[2] The European Box Office Awards of 1993 preferred the category 'low-budget', won that year by Bigas Luna's *Jamón, Jamón* (Moore 1993). *Screen International* writes, optimistically, that, topping the charts in both Spain and Italy and making some $6 million in Europe, Bigas (and his comrades Almodóvar and de la Iglesia) 'proved that European films can have a pan-European market despite their cultural specificity'; and that 'Spain is now rivalling France as the key producer of European films with an international market'. Elsewhere evidence is confusing: *Moving Pictures* reported in the same year on a trend for Japanese companies to invest in European art films and 'run up the flag of independence' (Hirsig 1993); while in 1994 the European Script Fund allocated loans for forty-nine script projects (Dunkley 1994). In 1994 also it was reported that 'US investors [were] back[ing] off speciality films', while European investment in independents was increasing (Dawes 1994). By 1995 the Sundance Film Festival had become the popular place to show new European independent films (Saperstein 1995), while the next year a European initiative was launched to set up a financing body for low-budget films by new directors (Duncan 1996). Meanwhile the European Film Distribution Office 'lobb[ied] for Euro indies' (Blaney 1996), while the European Film Academy held a seminar on how the European industry could learn from the independent industry in the USA (TTR 1996). While such reports replicate the terminological confusion of the US surveys (citing in turn 'low-budget', 'art' or 'speciality' films), they confirm the usefulness, and indeed the pervasiveness, of the term 'independent' even in a Europe whose conditions are so different from those in the USA, where the label was spawned.

Catalan cinema

What is known, what is remembered in the Spanish state of the past of Catalan cinema? Almost nothing.

(Centro de Investigaciones Film-Historia 1993: 7)

Hollywood Reporter has some difficulty with defining independents even in the USA, giving each producer in its 1997 special issue on the theme a 'report card' on indie status. Thus the makers of *The English Patient* (which grossed $78 million) are described in the following terms: 'A wholly owned subsidiary of the Walt Disney Co., Miramax is a self-contained entity responsible for the production, marketing, and distribution of its home grown and acquired fare' (*Hollywood Reporter* 1997: 16). Or again, the distributors of *Shine* ($36 million) are described thus: 'Set up to operate out of New York as a grass-roots indie label, Fine Line's distribution and marketing staff report to New Line . . . So Fine Line's "independence". . . is a relative point' (*Hollywood Reporter* 1997: 19).

If definition is so difficult in the USA, how much more so in Catalonia, a nation without a state where 'independence' necessarily goes beyond the aesthetic and economic to embrace the political dimension. And what is 'Catalan' cinema? A 'dictionary of directors' completed in 1993 distinguished carefully between 'Catalan cinema' (made in the language), 'cinema in Catalonia' (made by natives in either of the two official languages), and 'cinema made in Catalonia' (produced by those who have lived and worked there irrespective of their birthplace or native language) (Crusells and Sebastian 1993: 124–5).

The current state of Catalan cinema, however defined, is not a happy one. Of the new Spanish directors interviewed by Heredero (1997), a category that became increasingly numerous in the Nineties, only one of the fifteen (Isabel Coixet) is Catalan, and the best known of her two features is a film shot in New York and in English which seeks to reproduce exactly the US indie format. Catalan directors, both those firmly established, such as Bigas Luna, and those young and challenging, such as Marc Recha, have repeatedly attacked the Generalitat's subsidy policy. Recha, the uncompromising *auteur* of minimalist art movies in Catalan, claims that the authorities advised him to make westerns, and calls the Generalitat's Department of Culture 'those responsible for having destroyed Catalan culture, responsible for the most damaging ideological control of recent years, the promoters of a folksy regional cinema, of cheap farces and phony epics, worse than the cinema made under Franco' (Heredero 1999: 298). Rarely have the questions raised by Finney regarding the cultural and political effects of subsidy been put so bluntly.

Analysis of the trade press of the past decade suggests that the industrial effects of the Generalitat's policy have also been negative. At the start of the decade, as the Generalitat awarded prizes in recognition of local filmmakers' contributions to the film industry in Catalonia (*Cineinforme* 1990), *Screen International* gave a detailed report on the region's efforts to develop its audiovisual future in the domestic and international markets on the eve of the Olympic Games (Mitchell 1991). Asking 'Homage to Catalonia . . . or to Madrid?', *SI* compares the two rival regions. Although *SI* claims that 'Catalonia's film and television industry certainly mirrors the region's richness', and that Catalan-language TV-3 boasts a 'higher domestic production slate than the national network', it warns that 'few outside the region have heard of a Catalonian director or seen a Catalonian film'. And although 'regional government support is healthy', as is financial investment by Catalan banks, a major local distributor and producer went bankrupt in early 1991. Attempts are being made to overcome 'parochialism' ('a frequent criticism of Catalonian filmmaking') through such schemes as a publicly funded script-writing seminar with a US teacher. But what Catalonia lacks is 'a personality such as Pedro Almodóvar to give the region's film industry a greater credibility'. In contrast, Madrid is 'the centre of [Spain's] audiovisual industry' and 'the base for 60 per cent of film and television production'. Madrid's regional economic development trust IMADE has sponsored seminars on European co-productions with Eurimages; and 'because of its central location and strength, Madrid will undoubtedly remain the centre for the state industry, the home of the distribution majors such as UIP and Warner and headquarters for the booming independent networks'. Moreover, Madrid benefits from its position as a link between Iberia, Europe and Latin America.

Cineinforme documents attempts to transcend this continuing marginalization. In 1992 the Catalan Producers Association organized a production course in Barcelona (Anon. 1992); but the next year a hundred Catalonian cinemas faced closure for failing to comply with European Community exhibition quotas (by which cinemas had to devote one day in three to EC films) (Widdicombe 1993a). Meanwhile a $9 million discrepancy in Catalonia's reported box office take jeopardized subsidies for local producers (Widdicombe

1993b). A Madrid-commissioned report claimed that the Generalitat's policy of 'linguistic normalization' had weakened the industry;
that the subsidies to dub US films into Catalan were 'hypocritical';
and that there were 'doubts about the fairness and transparency'
of subsidy awards (Widdicombe 1993c). While the Generalitat per-
suaded central government to incorporate a measure to protect
Catalan language in its new film law (Widdicombe 1993d), problems continued. The region's biggest lab, Fotofilm, went bust
(Widdicombe 1994a); and a survey showed that only one-third of
films subsidized in 1986–92 recouped their public funding at the box
office, and that the audience for Catalan films fell from 6.5 million
in 1982 to 882,000 in 1991 (Widdicombe 1994b). The linguistic
debate continued throughout the decade, culminating in a year long
stand-off between the Generalitat and distributors until a decree
that all films shown in the region would be dubbed into Catalan was
finally withdrawn (*Cineinforme* 1999, 2000).

Beyond the invaluable but myopic perspective of the trade press,
however, scholarly research, overwhelmingly focused on the early
historical period of cinema, gives a quite different emphasis. Two
themes emerge. The first is the possibility (and brief historical
realization) of a Catalan cinema whose challenging aesthetic brief
echoes definitions of independent cinema elsewhere. The most
recent example of this is the Barcelona school of the 1960s. Joaquín
Jordá (a participating director in the movement) offers nine characteristics of the school: self-financing; team working; formal concern
for structure, image and narrative; experimental and avant-garde
character; subjective treatment of themes; characters and themes
independent of those of Madrid; non-professional actors; production unconcerned by prospects of distribution; and, finally, directors
lacking in formal training (Semana de Cine Español 1991: 13).
While the school's films were commercially disastrous and failed to
develop the sector (in the next decade Catalonia's share of employment in Spain's audiovisual industry fell from 24.89 per cent to
19.34 per cent) (Romaguera i Ramió 1986: 265, 268), the self-
conscious marginality and economic precariousness of the school
would be recognizable to Christine Vachon, doyenne of US indies.

A second, earlier moment reveals a different but related combination of catalanitat and independent aesthetics. Palmira González
López writes of the little-known 'art cinema' of the silent period.
As in the case of the school of Barcelona, such films may be more
interesting for their implications than for their intrinsic worth (1986:
48).[3] Based for the most part on Romantic drama, and not the more
radical trends of Modernisme, such films suffered from an excess of

theatricality and exploited the gestural style of well-known actors (49). But their intent was to elevate low-status cinema to the level of dramatic theatre, by choosing prestigious authors and a cast of celebrated actors that included Margarida Xirgu (49). The pioneer director was Fructuós Gelabert, adapter of Àngel Guimerà's *Terra Baixa* (1907) and *Maria Rosa* (1908) for Films Barcelona: 'The policy of *catalanitat* typical of "Films Barcelona" could not be clearer: it chose the best known and most loved of Catalan playwrights and, of their works, two that attempt to capture the distinctive character of the [Catalan] people' (49). In 1990 film scholars were still lamenting the paucity of literary adaptations in Catalan cinema (Minguet Batllori 1990: 140) and contrasting unfavourably the artistic poverty of cinema with the creative wealth of theatre in Catalonia (Romaguera i Ramió 1990: 164). The objective conditions of the Catalan cultural field, both industrial and artistic, thus made it possible for a truly independent Catalan cinema to emerge, one that combined both the school of Barcelona's aesthetic ambitions and autonomy from Madrid with Films Barcelona's appeal to the reassuringly prestigious authors and actors of Catalan drama. It was the strategy to be followed by the most consistent Catalan director of the 1990s: Ventura Pons.

Ventura Pons: the career

Born in Barcelona in 1945, Ventura Pons is the most critically and commercially successful director in Catalonia. His unique achievement is to have produced a substantial body of work, some ten features, in the Catalan language during a period when production in Spain in general (and in Barcelona in particular) has been under particular pressure from Hollywood. Now almost as regular in his creative rhythm as Woody Allen, Pons (like Allen again) lays claim to the status of *auteur*. His own producer with the independent Els Films de la Rambla (founded in 1985), he also shares screen-writing credits for his films with some of the best-known novelists and dramatists of Catalonia. Invariably intelligent and eloquent, and marked by a love of his native Catalan culture, of theatre, and of minimal narrative, Pons's cinema is also surprisingly varied. It ranges from the *vérité* documentary *Ocaña* to the self-conscious narrative of *What It's All About*, via farcical comedies such as *What's Your Bet, Mari Pili?* Unseen in Britain before his recent *Caresses* was shown at the ICA (although the earlier *Actresses* was seen at the London Film Festival in 1997), with the current retrospective Pons now stands revealed as a major European director who shows us how to make films in a small country.

(Smith 1998)

As one Catalan critic has noted, Ventura Pons's career is 'as surprising as it is important' (Gato 1998). After five comic features, popular in Catalonia but ignored or reviled outside, Pons shifted gear in the second half of the Nineties, producing literary adaptations which transcended local limits and won critical acclaim beyond his native country. The institutional prestige achieved by this shift up-market is evident. *El perquè de tot plegat* (*What It's All About*) marked Pons's award of the National Film Prize of Catalonia from the Generalitat (1996) (previously his features had won recognition only for their performances) and Pons's first nominations for the Spanish Goya prizes (in script and music); *Actrius* (*Actresses*, 1996) also won a Goya nomination, while *Caricies* (*Caresses*, 1997) marked the first time that Pons was admitted to one of the three major European festivals. Berlin went on to accept his two subsequent productions *Amic/Amat* (*Friend/Lover*, 1998) and *Morir (o no)* (*To Die or Not*, 1999). Head of the Catalan Col·legi de Directors in 1994, Pons was elected, after his career shift, vice-president of the Spanish Academia de Cine (1998) and received retrospectives in London and New York.

This career, lengthy and hard won, has been made under the sign of independence. An important interview with a sympathetic, but relatively ignorant, interlocutor at the Bogotá Film Festival of 1997 presents Pons to the Colombian public as 'a man with an independent vision' (Correa 1997: 9). Pons names his films since *El perquè* as the 'trilogy of risk': unconventional and anomalous, they are the result of a personal desire. And he sets out an individual and national history that is rigorously marginal. Proud to be his own producer, he claims that artistic independence had a high financial price: he had to mortgage his home to set up the company (10). Likewise, filmmaking in Catalonia is precarious in the extreme, cannot even be called a 'movement', let alone an industry (10). Pons rejects the 'aesthetic provocation' of the Barcelona school of the 1960s, although he understands its utility at the time (11); and he claims that Spanish cinema began in Catalonia and was destroyed after the Civil War with the relocation of the industry to Madrid (where the 'big studios' remain) and the long suppression of the Catalan language (11). While theatre remained relatively autonomous under Franco, because lower costs made it less of a financial risk to attempt to subvert censorship, cinema had, and has, to be seen 'in terms of the market'. Although films can now be made in Catalan, they still cannot recoup their costs in such a small territory. Eighty per cent of Pons's audience remains Catalan, while the 'natural' outlet for his products, the Spanish, remains barred. For Pons it is not the Catalans who are nationalists, but the Spaniards; and the 'problems' belong not to the former, but to the latter. Working in one's own language is not a political gesture, but simply a way of using one's own material ('lo que te resulta propio'). Spaniards claim that Catalans are forever waving their flags. But Pons claims that he 'hates' flags, and wishes simply to communicate, not to lecture his audience (11).

A recent book on Pons, published to coincide with a retrospective at the Huesca festival (Campo Vidal 2000), declares the 'freedom' of his vision. The indulgent author relates the key points of Pons's personal and professional narrative: his birth into a middle-income family in bleak, post-war Catalonia; his escape to London (an 'oasis of freedom') as an adolescent enthused by British Free Cinema and the Angry Young Men of the UK theatre (Campo Vidal 2000: 21); his early success as a theatre director (22–4); his particular concern for the direction of actors (25); his recurring themes (such as homosexuality, his 'trade mark' (27)); his love of a fully developed concept and a well-made script (28, 29) and his hatred of the dubbing to which Catalan cinema is subjected (30), and through which the US 'enemy' has been handed the great advantage of something 'so unique and personal as a language' (31). Advocating multiculturalism (31), Pons complains of the 'double competition' facing Catalan cineastes from both Hollywood and Madrid (33). Moreover, local critics are often unhelpful in this enterprise, failing to recognize the 'fragility' of cinematic labour (36).

With the stakes set against him, Pons's only defence is 'independent production (producir con independencia)' (34). Claiming that 'cinema is an industrial art, an artistic industry', Pons narrates his difficulties in setting up Els Films de la Rambla in 1985, and proudly defends the label of producer-director, which is sometimes scorned by the industry (34). He explains his reasons after failing to find finance after his first fiction feature *El vicario de Olot* (*The Vicar of Olot*, 1981), a localist comedy which launched the film career of frequent collaborator Rosa Maria Sardà:

> I had spent so many years trying to take that script forward that at that moment I took one of the most important decisions of my life. I realized that in order to be able to work freely and independently and to do my own projects I had to set up my own production company, because then I wouldn't be dependent on the decisions of people who neither understood me as a director, nor had a firm industrial grounding themselves. (48)

Aesthetic and commercial criteria are thus mutually reinforcing and inextricable.

Such an attitude would set Pons at odds with the developing policy of Spanish film funding. Indeed, as reforms were announced in 1994, he attacked the 'dangerous' new measures, claiming that there could be no 'free market' in an industry that remained subordinate to the interests of the US majors (Anon. 1994). But in his early years Pons claims to be as discriminated against by Barcelona as by Madrid, where subsidies were allocated on the basis of cronyism. And of course there was no absolute independence even for Pons's later films: like many of Vachon's US indies, they are pre-sold to distributors, in this case a shifting mosaic of regional, national and European TV companies (TV-3, TVE and Canal +). Further family resemblances to US indies are Pons's belief that actors are the single most important factor in films; his gamble on niche audiences (with 'gay films in Catalan' even less of a sure thing than *The Wedding Banquet*'s queer Cantonese); the aesthetic return to the formal simplicity of the masters (although Pons will cite Mankiewicz more readily than Ozu); and the cultivation of a specialized theatrical audience (only one-third of viewers even in Catalonia prefer pictures made like Pons's in the local language).

Within Spain, as noted earlier, Pons's penchant for art cinema goes against recent trends underlying the 'Spanish upswing'. While Madrid producers have tended to target more commercial projects in the Nineties than in the Eighties, and have sought to combine cultural specificity with pan-European appeal (a goal only fitfully realized), Pons has drifted ever further up-market and, through literary adaptations, placed his work firmly within the field of established Catalan culture. Gaining critical consecration at the cost of commercial success, Pons has benefited proportionately less than other filmmakers in the Spanish state from a subsidy system which now rewards the highest-grossing films the most generously. Indeed, official figures give the theatrical audience of his films as alarmingly small.[4]

In spite of Pons's professed distance from parochial Catalan cultural policy, then, his career raises in heightened terms the question of public funding posed by Finney: are subsidies given for short-term cultural, political and national purposes at the expense of longer-term industrial, commercial and international interests? While it is difficult to see how Pons's niche production can substantially reinforce a Catalan audiovisual sector that is in permanent crisis, the rise in international visibility prompted by Pons's presence at festivals such as Berlin is not to be dismissed out of hand: we remember that it is an established figure comparable to Almodóvar that *Screen International* claimed Catalonia most lacked. Moreover, Pons clearly does not merit the bitter criticism of a young director such as Recha: while Pons's early lumpen farces could indeed be accused of 'vaudeville', the later works avoid both folkloric regionalism and epic pretension. Close analysis of three features by Pons will show that the tensions we have seen between aesthetics and economics are played out in three related but distinct themes: homosexuality, literarity and urbanism.

Three films: *Ocaña, Actrius, Caricies*

The free vision.

(Subtitle of Campo Vidal 2000)

Ocaña

The production history of Pons's first feature, *Ocaña, retrat intermitent* (*Ocaña, an Intermittent Portrait,* 1977), is as heroic as any in the short history of no-budget US indies. Shot in just five days on 16 mm, a documentary about an Andalusian drag queen in Barcelona seemed destined for obscurity. According to Pons, however, it was a series of happy accidents which made this 'unpremeditated' film one of the greatest artistic and commercial successes (relative to its tiny budget) in all Spanish cinema. After the editor of *Interviú* magazine, the new sex and scandal sheet, was invited to a private screening, parent company Zeta paid for the film to be blown up to 35 mm. In Paris, by chance once more, Pons spoke to the Cannes press office (he himself had press accreditation), and *Ocaña* was picked up for the new non-competitive strand 'Un certain regard' (Campo Vidal 2000: 42). 'Apotheosic' screenings in Berlin and worldwide festivals followed (43).

Critics stressed two points: the transparency of Pons's style and the indexical quality of the film as testimony to its historical moment. Thus Fernando Trueba wrote in *El País* that the direction was 'direct, clear, unpretentious' (93), while Terenci Moix called the film 'the first authentic portrait of post-Franco Spain' (93). Now Francoism is definitively dead, a long repressed culture can be 'vomited up' without restraint (94). One distinguished critic who was consistently to champion Pons, José Luis Guarner, raised the question of the

13 Ventura Pons, *Ocaña* (1977). Courtesy of Films de la Rambla.

film's *catalanitat*: while only the credits are in Catalan (Ocaña speaks in his richly vernacular Andaluz), the film draws on a Barcelonan tradition of 'liberalism' that is exemplified by the 'totem' of the Rambla (94–5). It is curious indeed, then, that such a marginal film, devoted to a niche market as minute as that of immigrant drags in the Catalan capital, should come to bear the symbolic charge of representing the entirety of the Spanish state at a crucial historical moment.

Close analysis of *Ocaña*, however, reveals how the supposed transparency of the film, its undoubted attention to, and respect for, the everyday and the oral, is supplemented by a tendency toward the artificial and the aesthetic: in a word, the literary. The film crosscuts 'intermittently' but consistently between the interior of Ocaña's bedroom in which he narrates his life story to an unseen and unheard interlocutor (Pons himself) and diverse dramatic locations, often exteriors, which bear a shifting and sometimes problematic relation to the main narrative. There are fifteen oral or narrative segments and sixteen dramatic or illustrative segments (if we include the brief exteriors of the Plaça Reial and Rambla which open and close the film). The latter segments are sometimes explicitly literary. For example, Ocaña plays out fragments of popular plays in which, extravagantly dressed and posed on a tiny stage, he represents the stereotypical mourning mother or abandoned lover. These segments are revealed as yet more literary and self-conscious when we take into consideration Pons's claim that he himself discovered these popular dramas in the archives and encouraged Ocaña to perform them for the camera. The theatrical *mise en scène* is repeated in a more ambiguous context in those fragments where Ocaña performs in public space. Thus (again prompted by Pons) he sings a saeta in a mantilla from a balcony in Barcelona's Barrio Gótico. Another song is set in a cemetery (the camera essays rudimentary tilts and pans here), a third in the famous Café de l'Opera. Conversely, when Ocaña parades down the Rambla with friends Camilo and Nazario, in sun dress, floppy hat and no knickers, there is no live sound: the folkloric standard 'El torito bravo' plays over the sequence. The narrative nature of these songs, mini *mises en scènes* directly comparable to the theatrical fragments, points to the dependence of everyday life on the aesthetic, the shift from oral performance to literary competence.

The talking head interiors are graphically marked as distinct from these overtly theatrical numbers: Ocaña, perched on his bed, is discreetly dressed in white shirt, black hat and no make-up. But even here the natural or transparent merges into the artificial and opaque. Ocaña's life story, told in sequence, is highly novelistic, artfully constructed. His alienation from the restrictions of life in the pueblo; his burgeoning sexuality; his love of church ritual and for a youth who subsequently, claims Ocaña, was to commit suicide – all these are presented with engaging and eloquent, if loquacious, skill. Moreover, Pons supplements these confessions, apparently natural, with an unobtrusive but insistent repertoire of cinematic resources. Thus the talking head shots are elegantly varied: Pons begins now with a close-up of Ocaña's face, now with a long shot revealed, by a shaky pan, to be a reflection in the mirror on the wall, now with a detail of a painting from which he tilts down to the face once more. The camera pulls back to reveal Ocaña's expressive hands or in to focus on a variety of props: a cigarette, a fan and, in the final sequences, a photogenic black cat.

The cinematic resources of camera placement and movement (however vestigial) are thus combined with theatrical techniques of bodily expression and literary resources of narrative and reference. Furthermore, Ocaña sports a bewildering variety of looks throughout the film, from full folkloric drag to a stubbly, bespectacled appearance as he hangs his paintings for an art exhibition. The film thus problematizes identity even as it presents itself as a 'portrait'. And on closer analysis, the relationship between the confessional scenes and the exterior fragments is also subtly varied. Sometimes the latter are simply illustrative or analogical, triggered by a specific reference in Ocaña's narrative: thus his tender references to friends Camilo and Maria de la Rambla prompt brief shots of the former dancing sevillanas and the latter, clearly drunk or stoned, singing along to Piaf in a record store. Elsewhere the technique is contrastive or disruptive: Ocaña's account of the horrors of his childhood is cross-cut with his glory days as a very adult totem of the Rambla. The most problematic and complex case is that of homosexuality. While Ocaña voices a position typical of the period (the rejection of all labels: straight, gay or transvestite), a black-and-white montage of still photographs shows an early street demonstration by the Catalan gay liberation front (FAGC) and, climactically, luridly coloured footage of Ocaña's own performance at the PCC at which he tore off his flamenco dress to stand naked on-stage.

This swift, defiant and unerotic strip-tease reveals the peculiar significance of homosexuality, noted by all contemporary critics. Focusing on, but not addressed to, what must be one of the smallest and worst-defined communities imaginable, *Ocaña* transcends the singularity of its subject matter by revealing the theatricalization of politics in a newly dramatized society. Just as Ocaña's oral testimony is dependent on a literary script (rigorously researched by his director), so Pons's independence is only relative, the 'freedom of his look' underwritten by a dependence on a text that is performance in both the limited and the unrestricted senses. If Ocaña, self-proclaimed 'Pasionaria de las mariquitas [queers]' (Campo Vidal 2000: 40), still speaks to contemporary Spanish audiences, it is not simply the result of nostalgia for a golden age of transgression, but because *Ocaña*'s problematic and oblique politics of performance continues to hold the attention when the traditional politics of the Left, so rudely interrupted by Ocaña's strip-tease, have fallen so far from favour.

Actrius

If *Ocaña* is a disguised adaptation (appealing to literary precedent in both its confessional and dramatic fragments), *Actrius* is, to the contrary, a disguised documentary (revealing that even the most abstracted literary artifice is contaminated by the particularity of the everyday). This intertwining of the aesthetic and the social is clear in the production history of *Actrius*, so different from that of *Ocaña*. With his adaptation of fifteen Quim Monzó's stories, *El perquè de tot plegat* (1994), Pons had, according to *La Vanguardia*, 'experienced once more the recognition of both audiences and critics, something he had lacked since *Ocaña, retrat intermitent*' (Llopart 1996). Strengthened by this new-found artistic and industrial success, Pons planned a new, 'more intimate' film: *Actrius*, an adaptation of J. M. Benet i Jornet's *E.R.*, which had won the Teatro Nacional Prize the previous year after premiering at Barcelona's artistically renowned Teatre Lliure. While Pons no longer had problems with production (*El perquè*'s budget of 130 mill ptas had been met 50–50 by the Catalan Generalitat and the Spanish Ministry of Culture) (Gafarot 1994), he now encountered problems of reception. He himself wrote: 'With this film [*Actrius*] I begin to make a cinema with which I gain excellent reviews, but at the cost of gradually losing an audience' (75). Critical and commercial success seem irreconcilable given the youthfulness of cinema's public, who are unlikely to appreciate stories of older women reminiscing about their lives in the theatre. Audiences, writes Pons, have not been 'culturally nourished (alimentado)' to appreciate such rarefied fare (75).

Critical response was favourable but contradictory. Jordi Costa wrote in *Avui* (20 January 1997) that Pons had transformed the play into a piece of 'extremely pure cinema'. The filmmaker 'disappears', and the spectator enters into unmediated contact with the subject

14 Ventura Pons, *Actrius* (*Actresses*, 1996): the Girl (Mercè Pons, left) and Maria (Anna Lizaran). Courtesy of Films de la Rambla.

'in the most direct (frontal) manner possible, without formal filters or interference'. Conversely, M. Torreiro wrote in the Madrid edition of *El País* of the film's 'textual richness [which] is produced by a wealth of [literary] references', most obviously a fragment of *Iphigenia in Aulis* that is repeated three times in the film as the unidentified 'Girl' interviews the three older actresses of the title. *La Vanguardia* spelt out some cinematic references too: the toy theatre inherited by the Girl from mythical diva Empar Ribera (clearly based on the historical Margarida Xirgu) serves the same function as Welles's Rosebud (and is likewise reduced to ashes at the end); the confrontation between novice and star echoes Mankiewicz's *All About Eve* (Bonet Mojica 1997). As in *Ocaña*, then, transparency and opacity (orality and literacy) are fused in unstable combination.

The question posed by *E.R.* and *Actrius*, play and film, is precisely that of artistic independence: is pure art aesthetically autonomous, or is it contaminated by social and economic conditions? The three named protagonists thus exemplify somewhat schematically different positions in the cultural field. Glòria (Nuria Espert) is the critically acclaimed stage actress who has performed Greek tragedy in the shadow of the Acropolis; Assumpta (Rosa Maria Sardà) is the much-loved TV star who despises the sitcoms that have made her wealthy; and Maria is the unknown dubber whose labour is both critically and financially undervalued. The fact that all three shared the same mythical drama teacher and competed in their youth for the role of Iphigenia highlights the contingency of an artistic career, even as the symmetricality of the plot abstracts the narrative, encouraging us to worship at the 'monstrous' shrine of theatre to which the Girl too will willingly sacrifice herself.

As in *Ocaña*, then, the conflict between fiction and reality is already explicit in Pons's material. And, as in *Ocaña* once more, Pons complements theatrical *mise en scène* with cinematic resource. Thus the hermetic and abstracted sets of the play are initially opened up with a mobile camera. The play's prologue, in which the Girl recounts her childhood love of the toy theatre, is physically re-enacted for us in the film; and the Girl's initial confrontation with each of the three actresses is enlivened by appeal to additional spaces beyond the single set and simple props of the play. Thus Benet i Jornet economically evokes Glòria's workplace through sound (furious ovations) and 'a gaudy curtain hanging, half pulled back, from a wall' (Benet 1997: 9). Pons, on the other hand, follows the Girl as she enters the theatre, and proceeds with her through the auditorium on to the stage. Assumpta's workplace is signalled by the apparition of 'one of those machines that inhabit TV studios' (12), while Pons takes us from the crowded set down a corridor to the star's dressing room. Finally, Maria's dubbing studio is evoked with just 'a lectern with papers' (16). Pons tracks with the two women from this interior to a new exterior as they walk along the city street.

This desire, conventional enough, to open up a claustrophobic theatrical *mise en scène* with a more filmic spatial mobility is, however, contradicted by Pons's purist fidelity to Benet i Jornet's text. The six-scene structure is retained, the dialogue truncated but not transformed. But although critics have claimed that the central monologues of the play (in which each woman in turn gives conflicting accounts of their long-lost teacher) are presented without filters or interference, directly and frontally, they are in fact shot in a way that exhibits, albeit more smoothly, the same minimal cinematic syntax that Pons first attempted years earlier with *Ocaña*. Thus Pons tracks imperceptibly in and around his actresses as they continue their monologues, cross-cutting with the reaction of the avidly listening Girl. And, exploiting camera placement and movement, he also takes advantage of the basic props offered by Benet i Jornet: the bunch of flowers brought by the Girl to her interviewees, the whisky offered to her by each in turn. The very explicit symmetries of the text (the literal replaying of scenes with different protagonists, different performance styles) are thus re-created through analogous, but not directly related, visual patterns which unobtrusively direct and focus the spectator in ways clearly impossible on-stage. Moreover, emphasizing with close-ups our attention on individual women, Pons also uses framing to stress the relationship between pairs of them. At the end of the interview with diva Glòria, Pons holds Glòria and the Girl in a prolonged two shot, emphasizing their objective proximity and subjective distance: the older woman, enraptured by memories of her own triumph, remains oblivious to the Girl's requests for guidance on the reading of *Iphigenia* she has just attempted.

While such techniques are arguably commensurate with Benet i Jornet's theatrical minimalism, one aspect of Pons's *mise en scène* contrasts explicitly with it. This is Pons's use of cluttered, naturalistic sets. Glòria's flat, Assumpta's house and Maria's garden, obliquely sketched in a dramatic staging which retains the bare walls of the theatre throughout the piece, are in the film presented in their minute, distracting particularity. Moreover, the 'purity' of Pons's artistic vision is also undercut by one very knowing aspect of his film: its casting. The performances of Pons's actresses, none of whom appeared in the original production at the Teatre Lliure, were interpreted by spectators in relation to their real-life careers. Thus Benet i Jornet found it necessary to state that Sardà and Espert do and say things in the film that they would not in real life; and claimed, obscurely, not to have used real characters, but to have made use of them ('No he servido a personajes reales. Me he servido de personajes reales' (Pons and Benet i Jornet 1997)). The actresses themselves, in promotional interviews for the premiere, played according to type: the grand dame of the theatre Espert claiming that she had vowed never to make another film (Estrada 1997); the one-time sitcom queen Sardà (now appearing more frequently in film) expressing the same scorn for television as her character (Chamorro 1997). The hermetic reflexivity of Benet i Jornet (which culminates in the burning of the toy theatre on the real stage) is here translated into a different and more troubling kind of perspectivism, in which the tensions of the Catalan audiovisual sector are implicitly laid bare through the conflict between theatre and cinema, actress and star, performer and public figure.

It is perhaps no accident that the most perceptive critique of *Actrius*'s formal techniques (camera placement and movement) is also the most concrete in placing the play and film within the 'too fragile' sphere of Catalan drama (Bou and Pérez 1997). Pons's achievement is to prove the 'complementarity' of the three disciplines of theatre, cinema and television in producing a 'national imaginary'. Significantly, Benet i Jornet is cited as much in his role as creator of TV series drama *Poble Nou* as for being an established playwright, lighting the way for younger dramatists such as Sergi Belbel. Beyond parochialism and flag waving, then, Pons's subtle 'choreography' of the camera suggests 'a certain mobility in the stagnant waters of cinema policy', a new movement in a Catalan audiovisual sector which is by no means beyond criticism from its own press.

Carícies

Carícies was, on release, generally held to be the most ambitious and successful example to date of Pons's independent production and independent eye. Bou and Pérez praised once more Pons's 'productive encounter with other Catalan fiction-makers – novelists, short-story writers, playwrights –, with their everyday settings – most particularly the city of Barcelona' and Pons's 'notable stylistic evolution which has crystallised in powerful expressive minimalism' (Pressbook 1998). Terenci Moix, Catalan novelist and assiduous film fan, praised (in an ironic reference to Saint Teresa of Avila) Pons's 'path to perfection' (Pressbook 1998). Abroad, *Carícies* was Pons's first film to achieve theatrical distribution in the UK, thus paving the way for a retrospective. It also benefited from greater resources than Pons's earlier films, facilitating a large, prestigious cast of some twelve actors (including veterans Julieta Serrano and Rosa Maria Sardà and new star, Sergi López) and extensive and expensive night shooting on location in Barcelona.

Promoted systematically, but ambivalently, as the last in a trilogy from Pons on transcendental themes (with *El perquè* focusing on life, *Actrius* on death, and *Carícies* itself on love), *Carícies* continued the formal and thematic concerns of earlier films, thus enabling them to be recognized retrospectively as a coherent and consistent *oeuvre*. Hence *Carícies* features the now familiar minimalist narrative (eleven two-handed fragments), supplemented by technical versatility or virtuosity (the self-conscious appeal to a variety of shooting styles). In addition, *Carícies* extends Pons's exploration of diverse forms of sexuality (including lesbianism and suggested incest), literature (Sergi Belbel's source text is structurally based on Schnitzler's *La Ronde*) and the city (Barcelona is said by Pons to be the main 'character' of the film).

15 Ventura Pons, *Caricies* (*Caresses*, 1997): the Woman (Rosa Maria Sardà) and the Young Man (David Selvas). Courtesy of Films de la Rambla.

The paradox, however, is that this, the most characteristic of Pons's independent visions, is also the most dependent on the cultural capital of its source text, Belbel's play, which had been produced in Barcelona by the Generalitat's Centre Dramàtic in 1992 and exported throughout Europe (although not to the USA or UK) in the years preceding Pons's adaptation. Belbel's theatrical profile thus maps magically on to Pons's cinematic c.v. Belbel is known for his minimalist approach to all dramatic elements (plot, character, space, time and setting) (Gallén 1992: 7) and his formal versatility (ranging as he does from expressive experimentation to relative naturalism). And his thematic concerns, explored over some fifteen plays by *Caricies*, echo those of Pons: heterodox sex (in *Caricies*, a passionate embrace between two elderly women and an 'ambiguous' bath scene between father and son); literature (Belbel has incorporated references to Gide and Woolf in his plays and has directed works by playwrights from Molière to Beckett); and the city (treating the 'hard asphalt' and its themes of 'exclusion, poverty, and drugs') (Gallén 1992: 8). If Pons became *the* Catalan director of the 1990s, then Belbel was *the* dramatist at the start of the decade. *Avui* wrote quite simply: 'Catalan Theatre is Called Sergi Belbel' (cited in George and London 1996: 91).

Press coverage of Pons's adaptation stressed the parallells between the two artists, who promoted the film together from the start of production to the premiere, and are described as 'two creators with an international profile' (Rubio 1997). Pons, soon to be elected vice-president of the Spanish Film Academy, thus enhances the prestige of Belbel (it is his first work to be adapted for the screen) and is in turn elevated by association with a dramatist who is both 'young and consecrated' (*La Vanguardia* 1997). The mutual attribution of 'quality' (a term cited by reviewers (Hidalgo 1998)) is further facilitated by a process of inheritance, or the transmission of cultural and social capital from one generation to another: Belbel has directed works by Benet, whose minimalist practice he shares; Pons, producer of Benet, is introduced by Benet to Belbel.

This hermetic circularity is re-created within the form of the film itself, as is shown by the following synopsis:

Night in a big city. We witness eleven scenes of confrontation between couples, anonymous links in a chain of erotic violence. In an apartment a Young Man and Young Woman trade vicious blows as they discuss domestic trivia. In a deserted park the Young Woman meets the Elderly Woman, her mother, who is thinking of moving into a home. In the home the Elderly Woman dances with and kisses an Old Woman, who no longer remembers the affair the two once had. The Old Woman seeks out the Old Man (her brother), who has lived on the street since she stole his wife from him long ago. The Old Man is assaulted by a Kid, who recounts his wild escapades. The Kid returns home and invites the Man (his father) to join him in the bath, comparing penis sizes when he does. In a crowded railway station the Man breaks up with the Girl, brutally denouncing the foul smell of her vagina. The Girl angrily watches the Elderly Man as he prepares dinner in his flat. The Elderly Man visits the studio flat of the Boy, a male prostitute, bringing him the gift of a mirror in front of which he is fellated. Time now runs backwards to the moment when the film began. The Boy overhears the argument between the Young Man and Young Woman as he visits the Woman, his mother, in the flat below. He leaves after giving her money. The Young Man knocks at the Woman's door, asking to borrow cooking oil. Tenderly she caresses his battered and bleeding face.

Typically more faithful than the dramatist to the original work, Pons retains many of the pleasures of the play, most particularly the structural revelations produced by the juxtaposition of minimal scenes, links in the chain of disaffection and alienation. Thus the brutality of the Young Woman's treatment of her lover and mother (the Young Man and Elderly Woman, respectively) is later justified by the Elderly Woman's revelation that she always hated the daughter. Or again the Girl, who is so foully attacked by the Man, treats her father (the Elderly Man) with equal hostility. Such ironies, 'dramatic' in both senses of the word, are jealously preserved even as Pons experiments with cinematic technique: the first fragment is edited with rapid fire cuts matching the explosive dialogue; the second in a single, slow-tracking shot, circling a couple trapped in a less spectacular, if no less bitter, conflict. As in the adaptation of Bernet *Actrius*, Belbel's minimal props (a park is signalled by a stone bench, a street by a rubbish skip) are opened out by Pons through location shooting.

The main innovation here relates to the question of the city as *mise en scène*. For, while Pons claimed repeatedly in interview that he was aiming for a sense of claustrophobic enclosure, the diverse domestic interiors are linked by fast-motion subjective shots from a car speeding through neon-lit highways and subways. The velocity and volatility of these brief sequences suggest a violent abstraction of urban space that coincides with Belbel's laconic theatrical location, given at the start of the play as 'different spaces of a city' (Belbel 1992: 13). However, Pons's other innovation undermines this minimalist abstraction. The camera repeatedly returns to the distinctive revolving clock that is found in an emblematic central location: the Plaça de Catalunya.

Press coverage, once more, stressed the particularity of place in the film. Reports are filed from such diverse and variably recognizable locations as the main Sants railway station (Monedero 1997) and the streets of the Poblenou working-class suburb (Llopart 1997). Pons himself notes the peculiar pressures of shooting in the Catalan capital: the city's unfamiliarity with the needs of filmmakers and the difficulty and expense of gaining permissions. ·

I would argue that this precarious balance between abstraction and particularity is inherent in the notion of independent or niche cinema, most especially in Catalonia. The theme of urban alienation, supposedly universal in modern societies, forms part of a lingua franca which permits smaller nations to participate in dialogue with wider cultural currents (compare Belbel's references to Beckett and Pons's to Mankiewicz). Yet the appeal to such general motifs undermines those specific references on which minority cultures rely to recognize their own identity and to promote it to other, more confident cultures. Hence Belbel's and Pons's employment of an international idiom (minimalism) is curiously contaminated by localist vernacular (the former's idiosyncratic Catalan, the latter's unmistakable metropolis). To put it more simply: space becomes place. And it is precisely this particularity of reference that both promotes and restricts the cross-over potential of independent film, since the latter may be read by foreign audiences as either exotic escapism or parochial exclusiveness. It is not the least of such contradictions that a national capital prized by locals and tourists alike for its uniquely rich density and sociality, so different and superior to the symbolic impoverishment of Anglo-American conurbations, should be portrayed by two of its consecrated artists (and to the acclaim of Catalan critics) as the epitome of international urban anomie.

From niche to sliver

In 1998 I was invited to interview Ventura Pons, whom I had not previously met, on-stage at London's Institute of Contemporary Arts. The occasion was the first theatrical screening in the UK of one of his films, *Carícies*. Before a mainly Spanish audience, Pons proved an admirable ambassador for his own self-produced cinema and for Catalan film in general: affable, voluble and fluent in English. Encouraged by the favourable reception of *Carícies*, the ICA planned a Pons retrospective. At the press preview, at which I and fellow-academic and Spanish film specialist María Delgado spoke, the film screened was not, as planned, the late, elegant *El perquè*, a print of which was unavailable that day, but the early, grungy *Mari Pili*. Reception was mixed. Such unfortunate accidents control the fragile fate of foreign-language film on screens in English-language territories.

In Catalonia the longing for recognition, however qualified, in metropolitan markets abroad is shown by the fact that the mere showing of *Carícies* in London, or the success of *El perquè* in Paris, remain sufficient motive for coverage in the local press (*La Vanguardia* 1998; Martí 1997). And for scholars working in such a small field it is difficult to avoid disturbing the object of study by analysing it: the text I wrote for the retrospective was swiftly posted by Pons on his extensive website; and my name was invoked by the Spanish press as authority for continuing Catalan innovation in the audiovisual sector (Sartori 1999). A reflexive critical practice, as recommended by Bourdieu, thus becomes essential in such cases.[5]

One clear distinction between Pons's audience at home and that abroad is his reception and promotion within a gay context in the latter. Pons's UK theatrical and video distributors, Dangerous to

Know, who were responsible for the UK retrospective, deal exclusively in gay and lesbian films; US-based academics such as Jaume Martí Olivella (2000: 381) praise Pons for making queerness central to Catalan culture, an attitude almost unknown at home. There, only Terenci Moix (also cited by Martí Olivella) openly calls attention to this aspect of Pons's work, and even he speaks slyly of the 'connoisseurs' who will appreciate the attractions of *Caricies*'s young male newcomers. Linking sex and the city once more, Moix praises Pons for producing a new image of urbanism in Spanish cinema, different from the vulgarities of post-Almodóvar Madrid comedies that have long been dominant (Pressbook 1998).

In spite of this critical praise, both academic and journalistic, theatrical audiences for Pons's recent features have not increased. *Amic/amat* (a dramatic two-hander on a gay theme from Benet) and *Morir (o no)* (a micro-narrative with a twist from Belbel) did not play well in local cinemas.[6] Some critics, going against the general consensus, believe that the stylized, abstracted language of such source material is uncinematic, even stagy (Marinero 1998). It may also be the case that the 'phenomenological space' cited by one specialist as characteristic of Catalan drama (Feldman 1999: 477), relying as it does on the physical presence of the actor's body to the audience, is not easily transferred to cinema.

While niche films do not aim to recoup their budgets through theatrical exhibition (only one of the 'windows' used to show their product) and the value of minority cinema is as much symbolic as it is economic, there is currently a sense that the institutionalization of Catalan culture may be harming even its consecrated artists. At the most recent National Prize ceremony (in which Belbel received yet another award), Jordi Pujol was uncharacteristically defensive, claiming that Catalan culture had not lost its vitality (*El País* [Barcelona] 2000). Yet Quim Monzó, another of Pons's collaborators, made a much-discussed speech of acceptance, claiming to have long expected such an award and suggesting, ironically, that the tediously extended ceremony was the best programme ever shown on TV3, the Generalitat-supported, Catalan-language network (Moliner 2000).

As Pujol and Monzó spoke, the largest chain of exhibitors in Barcelona was showing in the week of the Diada, or national day, fourteen films, of which only two were Spanish, and not one Catalan (Grup Balaña 2000). And in recent interviews Pons has continued to lament the absence of industrial acumen in Catalonia, while claiming that there is in principle no difference between this national cinema and that of the Danes or Hungarians (Piedrabuena 1998: 31). The paradox, as we have seen, is that Pons's laudable stress on aesthetic autonomy (his refusal to base artistic decisions on commercial criteria) has led in practice to increasingly universalizing accounts of sex, literature and the city. He has constructed a distinctive but highly abstract filmic space which is now far indeed from the messy, vibrant particularity of place he pioneered with *Ocaña*.

Christine Vachon, indie producer, fears that too much money talk 'demystifies' movies (1998: 17). For Bourdieu, on the other hand, demystifying the supposed independence of art from industry leads to a margin of 'freedom' for the newly enlightened citizen (1996: 340). And if niche production is clearly under threat, business has thrown up a new paradigm which might better serve the independent film sector: that of the 'sliver' (Marsh 2001). Sliver companies, also known as micro-multinationals, market 'a narrow range of products on a world scale'. Small, innovative, internet-skilled and fluent in English, slivers coincide precisely with the profile of Pons's Films de la Rambla, which sells a highly specialized product in tiny quantities to consumers in many countries. The *Financial Times* notes that micro-multinationals are often based in Europe (thereby suggesting that this is an area in which the Old Continent can compete successfully), and that they can operate 'without partnership with larger companies'. If the sliver model can provide no answer to the aesthetic cul-de-sac which Pons seems to have entered, it may help to explain the continued commercial existence of a valuable, vulnerable filmmaker who has survived against all the odds.

Notes

1 See especially Bourdieu 1996: *passim*.
2 See Bloom 1993 for an account of European independents from a US perspective.
3 See also Caparrós Lera 1993.
4 *Actrius*, 47,162 spectators, and *Carícies*, 58,812. *Ocaña* had gained an audience of 97,453 (www.mcu.es/cgi-bin/; consulted 19 July 2000).
5 My thanks are due to Ventura Pons and his staff for providing books, videotapes and stills; and to my former graduate student Sally Faulkner, specialist in literary adaptations.
6 The official Spanish ministry website gives 76,276 spectators for the first, 31,318 for the second (www.mcu.es/cgi-bin/; consulted 19 July 2000).

References

Anon. (1992) Los productores catalanes organizaron un curso de formación. *Cineinforme*, 621 (January), p. 38.

—— (1994) Ventura Pons critica el sistema de ayudas al cine. *El Periódico: Espectáculos*, 21 September, p. 56.

Belbel, Sergi (1992) *Carícies*. Barcelona: Edicions 62.

Benet i Jornet, Josep Maria (1997) *E.R.* Barcelona: Edicions 62.

Blaney, Martin (1996) EFDO to Lobby for Euro Indies. *Screen International*, 1071 (16 August), p. 3.

Bloom, Phillipa (1993) Overseas Subsidies. *Hollywood Reporter*, 328 (13) (August), pp. 11, 108–14, 116.

Bonet Mojica, Lluís (1997) Actrices con mucho teatro. *La Vanguardia*, 19 January, p. 61.

Bou, Núria and Pérez, Xavier (1997) 'Actrius' a la Ventura. *Avui: Espectacles*, 19 January, p. 54.

Bourdieu, Pierre (1996) *The Rules of Art*. Cambridge: Polity.

Campo Vidal, Anabel (2000) *Ventura Pons: la mirada libre*. Huesca: Festival de Cine de Huesca.

Caparrós Lera, J. M. (1993) El cine catalán durante la Renaixença. In Centro de Investigaciones Film-Historia 1993: 11–38.

Centro de Investigaciones Film-Historia (ed.) (1993) *El cine en Cataluña: una aproximación histórica*. Barcelona: PPU.

Chamorro, Coral (1997) Rosa Maria Sardà: 'Primero soy persona, luego actriz catalana'. *Cambio 16: Cine*, 3 February, p. 82.

Cineinforme (1990) Premios a los profesionales del cine en Cataluña. *Cineinforme*, 575–6 (February), p. 28.

—— (1999) La ley del mercado terminará imponiéndose en Cataluña. *Cineinforme*, 705 (January), p. 46.

—— (2000) El polémico decreto sobre el doblaje al catalán será retirado. *Cineinforme*, 719 (March), p. 58.

Corbett, Andrea (1999) The State of Independence. *Vertigo* [London], 9 (Summer), pp. 16–20.

Correa, Julián David (1997) Entrevista con Ventura Pons: un director en zapatillas. *Kinetoscopio*, 41, pp. 8–11.

Costa, Jordi (1997) Made in Heaven [review of *Actrius*], *Avui*, 20 January, p. 37.

Crusells, Magí and Sebastian, Jordi (1993) Diccionario de directores de cine en Cataluña. In Centro de Investigaciones Film-Historia 1993: 123–206.

Dawes, Amy (1994) US Investors Back Off Specialty Films. *Moving Pictures International*, 172 (10 February), p. 2.

Duncan, Celia (1996) Broadcasters Plan Euro Fund. *Screen International*, 1043 (2 February), p. 8.

Dunkley, Cathy (1994) European Script Fund Allocates Loans for 49 More Projects. *Moving Pictures International*, 172 (10 February).

Estrada, Cristina (1997) 'Hace tiempo que dejé el cine porque no lograba implicarme' [interview with Nuria Espert]. *Ya: Espectáculos*, 17 January, p. 44.

Feldman, Sharon (1999) 'Un agujero sin límites': la mirada fenomenológica de Josep M. Benet i Jornet. *Anales de la Literatura Española Contemporánea*, 24, pp. 473–91.

Finney, Angus (1996) *The State of European Cinema: A New Dose of Reality*. London: Cassell.

Gafarot, Xavier (1994) Ventura Pons llevará al cine los relatos de Quim Monzó. *Diario 16*, 5 July, p. 53.

Gallén, Enric (1992) Un model de literatura dramàtica per als noranta. In Belbel 1992: 5–9.

Gato, Gustavo (1998) Carícies. *Diari de Balears*, 24 February, p. 38.

George, David and London, John (1996) *Contemporary Catalan Theatre: An Introduction*. Sheffield: Anglo-Catalan Society.

González López, Palmira (1986) *Història del cinema a Catalunya*, vol. 1: *L'època del cinema mut, 1896–1931*. Barcelona: Els llibres de la Frontera.

Grup Balaña (2000) *Els cines i teatres de Barcelona* [exhibition schedule], 28 (8–14 September).

Heredero, Carlos F. (1997) *Espejo de miradas: entrevistas con nuevos directores del cine español de los noventa*. Alcalá de Henares: Festival de Cine.

—— (1999) *20 nuevos directores del cine español*. Madrid: Alianza.

Hidalgo, Manuel (1998) La trilogía de Ventura Pons. *El Mundo* [Madrid], 7 March, p. 12.

Hirsig, Andrea (1993) Japanese Film Backers Run Up Flag of Independence. *Moving Pictures*, 146 (29 July), p. 2.

Hollywood Reporter (1997) 348 (31) (5 August) [special issue on independent film].

Llopart, Salvador (1996) Entrevista a Ventura Pons, director de cine. *La Vanguardia*, 14 January, p. 53.

—— (1997) Ventura Pons finaliza el rodaje de 'Carícies', su décima película. *La Vanguardia*, 23 August, p. 28.

MacDonald, Scott (1998) *A Critical Cinema 3: Interviews with Independent Filmmakers*. Berkeley: University of California Press.

Marinero, Francisco (1998) Monólogos encadenados [review of *Carícies*], *Metrópoli* [Madrid], 27 February, p. 24.

Marsh, Peter (2001) A Little Goes a Long Way [report on 'niche companies'], *Financial Times*, 4 January, p. 11.

Martí, Octavi (1997) Éxito en París del filme de Ventura Pons sobre unos relatos de Monzó. *El País: Cultura* [Madrid], 8 April, p. 37.

Martí Olivella, Jaume (2000) Ventura Pons o la teatralització de la impostura. In Josep Anton Fernàndez (ed.), *El gai saber: introducció als estudis gais i lèsbics*, Barcelona: Llibres de l'Índex, pp. 373–92.

Minguet Batllori, Joan M. (1990) La ausencia de referentes culturales autóctonos en el cine producido en Cataluña. In Romaguera i Ramió, pp. 131–42.

Ministerio de Cultura (2000) www.mcu.es/cgi-bin/ [website with current film grosses]. Consulted 19 July.

Mitchell, Angus (1991) Homage to Catalonia . . . or to Madrid? *Screen International*, 802 (12 April), p. 14.

Moliner, Empar (2000) Vistiplau: Muñoz i Monzó, *El País: Quadern*, 14 September, p. 6.

Monedero, M. (1997) El rodatge de 'Carícies' mobilitza l'Estació de Sants. *Avui*, 17 August, p. 42.

Moore, Oscar (1993) European Box Office Awards. *Screen International*, 900 (26 March), p. 25.

El País [Barcelona]: *Cataluña* (2000) Pujol niega que haya un descenso de la vitalidad cultural en la entrega de los premios del sector, 11 September, p. 5.

Piedrabuena, Celes (1998) Entrevista a Ventura Pons, director de cinema. *El Temps*, 31 August, pp. 29–31.

Pierson, John (1995) *Spike, Mike, Slackers, and Dykes*. London: Faber & Faber.

Pons, Ventura and Benet i Jornet, Josep Maria (1997) Cuando el teatro entra en el cine. *El Mundo: Cinelandia*, 1 February, p. 8.

Pressbook to *Carícies* (1998) London: ICA (unpaginated).

Romaguera i Ramió, Joaquim (1986) *Història de la Catalunya cinematogràfica*. Barcelona: Federació Catalana de Cine-Clubs.

—— (1990) Literatura y cine en Cataluña. In *Hora actual del cine de las autonomías del estado español*, vol. 2: *Encuentro de la Asociación Española de Historiadores del Cine*, San Sebastián: Filmoteca Vasca, pp. 143–65.

Rubio, Teresa (1997) Pons lleva al cine 'Carícies', de Belbel. *El Periódico de Cataluña*, 17 June, p. 58.

Saperstein, Patricia (1995) Sundance Kids. *Moving Pictures*, 6 (February), pp. 33–5.

Sartori, Beatrice (1999) 'Me interesa el cine en el que se expresen ideas, aunque sean negativas' [interview with Pons], *El Mundo*, 6 January.

Semana de cine español (ed.) (1991) *La Escuela de Barcelona*. Murcia: Editora Regional.

Smith, Paul Julian (1998) Ventura Pons at the ICA. In *Ventura Pons: Retrospective* [programme], London: ICA (unpaginated).

Torreiro, M. (1997) ¡Qué señoras! [review of *Actrius*]. *El País* [Madrid], 25 January, p. 27.

TTR [*sic*] (1996) Europas Film muss lernen, *Film-Echo/Filmwoche*, 45 (9 November), p. 16.

Vachon, Christine (1998) *Shooting to Kill*. London: Bloomsbury.

La Vanguardia, (1997) Ventura Pons inicia el rodaje de 'Carícies', la pieza teatral de Sergi Belbel, 23 July, p. 41.

—— (1998) El filme 'Carícies' de Ventura Pons, se exhibirá en Londres, 17 June, p. 52.

Widdicombe, Rupert (1993a) Over 100 Catalonian Cinemas Face Closure for 6 Months for Failing to Comply with European Community Exhibition Quotas. *Screen International*, 898 (12 March), p. 4.

—— (1993b) A $9Million Discrepancy in Catalonia's 1991 Box-Office Take Could Result in Reduced Subsidies for Spanish Producers. *Screen International*, 900 (26 March), p. 2.

—— (1993c) Report Slams Catalonia Film Policy. *Screen International*, 906 (7 May), p. 8.

—— (1993d) Language Lobby Wins Protection. *Screen International*, 937 (10 December), p. 4.

—— (1994a) Catalonia's Fotofilm Goes Bust. *Screen International*, 946 (25 February), p. 2.

—— (1994b) Probe Rocks Catalan Funding. *Screen International*, 955 (29 April), p. 3.

6   Resurrecting the Art Movie? Almodóvar's Blue Period

The art movie

Art Movies: Overkill or Over-the-Hill?

(Cox and Bing 2000: 1)

Industry, critics and theorists have latterly coincided in proclaiming the death of the art movie. Thus a recent *Variety* cover article asked, 'Is the arthouse really dead? Or is it just playing possum?' (Cox and Bing 2000: 1). Since 1990, US arthouse box office has declined by 31 per cent. Paradoxically, however, 'studio presence has grown exponentially', with all the majors setting up specialized production outfits. *Variety* distinguishes arthouse from 'niche pictures' that are 'target[ed] to certain audiences on a limited scale such as ethnic-themed titles' (62). It defines arthouse on the basis of distribution ('any indie specialty title that opens on fewer than 600 screens'); and puts much of the blame for the decline of the genre on exhibition (even in 'top urban markets' such as New York and Chicago, multiplexes have a tough time selling arthouse titles). But production plays its part too. *Variety* writes that 'those pics have lost their identity': once 'the only place to see films dealing with sexual topics . . . art-house share started declining once those themes entered the mainstream via American films and TV shows'. Moreover, 'there are no Fellinis, Truffauts or Kurosawas to ignite the market' (1). Foreign films declined at the US box office from a high of 7 per cent in the 1950s to the current 1 per cent. Prestigious foreign directors, preferably with an interest in 'sexual topics', were thus in short supply in the 1990s.[1]

This industrial debate was anticipated by critics. Controversy broke out over the 1999 Cannes jury awards which favoured exceptionally austere art movies (*L'Humanité, Rosetta*) over more accessible fare (*Todo sobre mi madre* (*All About My Mother*)). A conference for critics, directors and distributors held at London's Institute of Contemporary Arts in October 1999 claimed that the Cannes debate 'suggest[ed] a growing divergence between art film and commercial cinema', with the former 'becoming increasingly marginal, its distributors and exhibitors an endangered species'. The ICA asked: 'Do independent filmmakers no longer have the vision to produce works which engage with a wider audience? Or has that audience been buried under a barrage of global marketing from the media conglomerates?' (ICA 1999). The latter view was put forcefully by Michel Ciment, member of the editorial board of *Positif*, who was nostalgic for the days when unquestionably great European *auteurs* filled theatres world-wide.[2] But most delegates argued that both industrial and cultural factors made the very definition of 'art cinema' increasingly difficult. Changes cited for the last two decades include the independents' loss of control over distribution and exhibition, a 'change in attitude towards an idea of "Art Cinema"', the shifting role of state subsidy, the homogenization of cultural 'product', and, finally, 'the proliferation of new forms of leisure activities' (ICA 1999). Such factors suggest that, given the current configuration of audiovisual industry and culture, there can be no return to the golden age of Fellini or Truffaut, directors cited, ironically enough, by both *Variety* and the Hollywood-hating Ciment.

This change in the attitude towards art cinema, apparently invisible to old school auteurists such as Ciment, is reinforced by current trends in critical theory. While postmodernism has long contested the division between high and low culture, powerful sociological models also problematize the very notion of the aesthetic and its supposed separation from the commercial. For Pierre Bourdieu, 'art' is a tautological category, granting itself cultural distinction through an aesthetic 'autonomy' which is the effect, not the cause, of its self-exclusion from the everyday. Bourdieu's notion of the cultural field, which I examine in my book *The Moderns* (Smith 2000b), requires us to examine simultaneously, and in their mutual constitution, texts, producers and institutions. Moreover, it strips the innocence from the cultural consumer, revealing the social investments implicit in, but rigorously excluded from, judgements of taste and value.

Paradoxically, however, the art movie also marks a point of rupture in Bourdieu's thought, in which his characteristic critique of the class basis of social capital is superseded by an attack on 'neo-liberalism' or globalization in the audiovisual sector. Questioning in *Le Monde* 'the real masters of the world' to be found in Hollywood (Bourdieu 1999), he defends the French film policy of cultural exception which historically has fostered just those established values of high culture that he has spent so many years demystifying.

Spanish art movies

> We are absolutely dependent on the exhibition sector.
>
> (Marisa Paredes, in Green 2001)

The question of Spanish art movies might seem to be tautological. As we have seen, for *Variety*, arthouse and 'foreign films' are almost synonymous. In a Spanish audiovisual market in which theatrical box office is split in a typical year between 85 per cent US film and 15 per cent local, it could be argued that Hollywood *is* popular Spanish film, and that choice local fare is a minority of a minority. The identity of any putative Spanish art movie is thus doubly lost, marginalized by both genre and national origin. Recent research suggests that when Spaniards decide to visit a cinema, they take for granted the fact that theatrically screened films are North American. As we shall see, the distinctive choice of a Spanish film is a conscious, minoritizing one, based on specific criteria rather than a generic preference for the medium as a whole.

Clearly, as in the case of the disappearing US art movie, such consumer 'choices' are determined by changing patterns of distribution and exhibition. Marisa Paredes, Almodóvar's distinguished leading lady, did not hesitate when elected president of the Spanish Film Academy to blame distributors for the peculiar plight of the industry in 2000: while, exceptionally, more than a hundred feature films were produced, the box office take fell from the previous year (Green 2001). Historically, 'cine de arte y ensayo' was a category fostered by the late Francoist technocrats, anxious to change Spain's image abroad through festival screenings of oblique and austere films (quintessentially Víctor Erice's *El espíritu de la colmena* (*The Spirit of the Beehive*)), whose distribution was carefully controlled at home.

If these elements contrive to alienate any Spanish art cinema from its supposed home, structural aspects of the audiovisual sector suggest, to the contrary, a more fertile field for the genre than might be expected. In the 1980s the main casualties of the precipitous fall in production, due in part to the shifting role of state subsidy, were popular genres: cheap exploitation pictures or the sex comedies that had typically starred such broad comedians as Alfredo Landa. Press critics in Spain are unusually institutionalized, displaying exceptional continuity and homogeneity. Ángel Fernández Santos, scriptwriter of *El espíritu de la colmena* and as well disposed to art movies as he is hostile to Almodóvar, has remained chief film critic at the dominant daily *El País* for some twenty years, even installing his daughter as second stringer. Likewise, Spanish theorists of film, frequently faithful to abstract and technical codes of structuralist narratology, have rarely rehabilitated popular filmmakers, choosing rather to lionize high art directors. In Bourdieu's terms, the Spanish cinematic field remains highly distinctive, with texts, producers and institutions combining and continuing to valorize high aesthetic qualities in a way that is not characteristic of other European territories, such as the UK.

Furthermore, while Michel Ciment, say, is nostalgic for the *auteur* era, the Spanish press has proved remarkably compliant in promoting new generations of directors to its public. Even relatively difficult directors, such as Julio Medem, have benefited from this blurring of the divide between art film and commercial cinema, which have, as we saw, diverged so widely elsewhere. For example, there is evidence that Spanish cinema has, with the help of the print media, begun to evolve a successful star system: unlike the more acerbic British media, critical of local product, the Spanish press is remarkably pliant in promoting successive 'generations' of actors in domestic films. Given that the lack of a European star system is generally held to be responsible for the relative failure of local production, such a development is not to be underestimated.

Exhibition also plays an ambivalent role here. *Variety* claims that in the USA, major urban markets are the natural, albeit endangered, habitat of the art movie. In Spain the exhibition sector has been transformed in the last decade with the closure of ailing theatres in rural areas and the proliferation of multiplexes in city centres.[3] Cinema attendance has become the privilege of rising numbers of relatively wealthy, educated and urban consumers. The tastes and values of such clients will not always be satisfied by Hollywood. Indeed, the conscious choice required to attend a Spanish film in Spain favours films with distinctive qualities that rise above the generic flow of North American cinema, now fully identified with the medium as a whole.

Let us, then, test the following hypothesis: in spite of the apparent hostility of the Spanish audiovisual environment to art movies (including the ready availability of 'sexual topics' once confined to the arthouse in the hard-core pornography that receives unusually wide distribution in Spain), the cinematic sector has recently reconfigured itself in such a way as to promote and protect precisely those characteristics of local production which correspond to the art movie profile. We can now look more closely at that profile in two areas: the divergent reception of foreign and domestic product and the convergent consumption of cinema and literature.

It is a rare and fortunate occurrence that we have reliable data on Spanish cinema attendance in the late 1990s. Undertaken by the Sociedad General de Autores y Editores (SGAE) and published in 2000, a survey on 'habits of cultural consumption' examines both objective conditions and subjective dispositions for Spanish cultural industries. We learn, for example, that the most assiduous cinema spectators (attending theatres more than twice a month) belong to the 'upper and upper middle class', have 'higher university degrees', and live in cities with over 30,000 inhabitants (78). Such spectators also volunteer the highest index of interest for film as a medium. Moreover, these tendencies increase year on year, showing a noticeable rise from 1997 to 1998. Inversely, but logically, lower social classes who rarely visit cinemas give the following reasons for their absence: satisfaction with films on TV, the high price of tickets, and the absence of, or distance from, cinemas in their place of residence (81).

Factors influencing the choice of film are more complex. North American films are selected (if indeed they are consciously selected at all) on the basis of the subject matter or plot, global promotion, or suitability for children. Domestic films are chosen, rather (and of course much more selectively), for the positive press reviews they have received and for the spectator's familiarity with the actors and/or director (90). The SGAE thus finds, to its surprise, that the shared national origin of filmmaker and audience brings no community of interest where subject matter is concerned. On the contrary, Hollywood themes (given typically as 'extraterrestrials, dinosaurs, and shipwrecks' (89–90)) are readily perceived as global 'events' by Spanish audiences. In addition, the minority of Spaniards who appreciate local production are polarized. Spanish films are, paradoxically, highly valued by those who 'practically never go to the cinema' as well as by those relatively well-educated and wealthy audiences who swelled attendances in the 1990s. The solution to this conundrum is found, once more, at the level of distribution.

Poor, rural audiences are condemned to view second-run Spanish films on free-to-air TV. Rich, urban spectators actively choose first-run films at the newly modernized city screens, to which they are attracted by press recommendation, peer word of mouth, or their own painfully acquired cultural capital: a distinctive taste for specific directors and actors who are, in turn, promoted by a press that is oriented to the middle classes (88–9). Distinct choices (of filmmaker or star) also correspond positively with indexes of cinema attendance (90).

Demographic data thus suggest, paradoxically once more, that commercially successful Spanish films will tend to be artistically distinctive, since the less demanding audiences are either too poor, ignorant and distant to visit a cinema at all or readily satisfied by the extraterrestrials and dinosaurs of Hollywood which exhaust their infrequent and intermittent experience of cinema. How, then, does this changing pattern of cinema viewing compare with the reception of that other endangered medium of cultural consumption, literature?

According to the SGAE, the habit of reading books, unlike that of going to films, has suffered a slow but sure decline throughout the 1990s (164). However, while occasional readers have fallen victim to 'audiovisual competition in the home', habitual readers (those who practise their art every day) have remained constant at 20 per cent of the population, namely those who have higher university degrees, are aged between 25 and 35, and belong to upper and upper-middle classes (164). Crucially also, these daily readers are predominantly women. Whereas readers of the daily press (only 30 per cent of the population, once more with middle or higher educational qualifications) are mainly male, they are sharply differentiated according to the sections they prefer, with female readers favouring social and cultural coverage, including 'film reviews'. Likewise women are the majority readers of monthly magazines.

Cross-referencing with film audiences of the 1990s, we see a close correspondence between the two demographics. Even the small dominance of male over female spectators in total cinema audiences is progressively diminished when it comes to minority and Spanish film: women consistently rate Spanish and other European films higher, and US films lower, than their male counterparts. It thus follows that a crucial opportunity opens up for Spanish filmmakers: the emergence of an educated, literate public proportionately more female and more interested in reading about film and in acquiring knowledge about directors and actors. This public is dissatisfied both with the homogeneous US product that still dominates Spanish cinema screens and with the local films shown free-to-air on TV:

they would rather read a book, selected sections of the newspaper, or choice magazines than watch Spielberg's dinosaurs or Alfredo Landa's beach bikinis. For this choice female demographic, then, literarity will be a select sign of preference, even in the audiovisual sector.

Almodóvar: three films

Toutes en scène.

(Ostria 1999: 35)

It has become a commonplace that Almodóvar's career can be divided into two unequal halves: the first ten features and the last three. The shift between the two is felt both objectively as a formal difference in cinematic style and subjectively as a career progression. Thus filmic extravagance gives way to austerity, and directorial innocence to experience. In a cover feature, respected French arts magazine *Les Inrockuptibles* describes the career shift as from 'période rose plus olé olé et période bleue plus austère et mature' (Ostria 1999: 33).[4]

While the description clearly raises questions of appeal to stereotypes of Spanishness that are problematic, it does coincide with certain trends in Almodóvar's cinema in relation to at least three themes: sex, literature and the city. Thus the early focus on sexual dissidence is replaced (in *La flor de mi secreto* (*The Flower of My Secret*) of 1995 and *Carne trémula* (*Live Flesh*) of 1997 at least) by a new attention to the problems and pleasures of heterosexuality; an early spontaneity, even improvisation, of narrative and dialogue gives way to a much more self-conscious literarity and appeal to texts as precedents; and finally, an optimistic vision of the city as setting for desire gives way to a more pessimistic view of urban life as the location of alienation, violence and AIDS.

Now I would suggest that *Les Inrockuptibles*'s division is simplistic (indeed, Almodóvar himself rejects it in the interview that follows). As I argued in the first edition of *Desire Unlimited* (published before the 'blue period' in 1994), Almodóvar's early films, widely dismissed as kitsch or camp, are uncompromising in their treatment of sombre themes: the impossibility of the couple, the irrevocability of loss, the persistence of trauma. *Entre tinieblas, La ley del deseo, Tacones lejanos* (*Dark Habits* (1983), *The Law of Desire* (1987), *High Heels* (1991)) all end in death and/or irredeemable solitude. Conversely, the final trilogy treats the theme of resurrection: in *La flor* Leo rises

16 Pedro Almodóvar: *La flor de mi secreto* (*The Flower of My Secret*, 1995): Leo (Marisa Paredes). Photo: Jean-Marie Leroy. Courtesy of El Deseo SA.

17 Pedro Almodóvar: *Carne trémula* (*Live Flesh*, 1997): Víctor (Liberto Rabal). Photo: Daniel Martínez. Courtesy of El Deseo SA.

18 Pedro Almodóvar: *Todo sobre mi madre* (*All About My Mother*, 1999): Manuela (Cecilia Roth, left) and Rosa (Penélope Cruz) at the Hospital del Mar. Photo: Teresa Isasi. Courtesy of El Deseo SA.

from the near death of her suicide attempt and establishes new, more promising relationships; in *Carne* the child Víctor, abandoned by mother and father, becomes a proud parent himself; and in *Todo sobre mi madre* (1999) the new-born Esteban triumphs over HIV to replace the lost brother and father of the same name. I would argue, then, that in spite of the redirection in focus and tone there remains a significant continuity of interest in Almodóvar's cinema.

What fascinates me about the model of rose and blue periods is, rather, the reference to art history and the career of Picasso. What I will argue is that the artistic and commercial success of Almodóvar's recent trilogy derives from his resurrection of the category long given up for dead: the art movie. How, then, does Almodóvar fit into this triple debate we have seen on art cinema: industrial, critical and theoretical? Not for the first time, he proves to be an anomaly. Industrially, his recent films are the exception to the rule. *Variety* cites *Todo sobre mi madre* as one of the 'string of speciality hits' distributed in the USA by Sony Pictures Classics (Cox and Bing 2000: 63); and *Carne trémula* was the second biggest foreign-language film of the year in the UK. And if the Oscar-winning *Todo* was denied the major prizes at Cannes, it was still the popular hit of the festival and garnered respectful coverage in the likes of *Cahiers du Cinéma*. Critically acclaimed, Almodóvar's new kind of arthouse also responds to theoretical changes in film culture. Neither too challenging, nor too simple, it combines in dynamic equilibrium increased measures of both aestheticization and social commentary. Resurrecting the art movie, Almodóvar thus enters into political debate, like Bourdieu's engaged intellectuals of the nineteenth century, as an autonomous artist whose position is at once legitimated and undermined by his scorn for party politics (Bourdieu 1996: 129–30).

This debate on cultural capital or distinction is incorporated quite explicitly into the fabric of the blue period pictures. *La flor* stages the conflict between 'pink' and 'black': that is to say, between popular romantic fiction and novels that are serious in both senses (high in status and melancholic in tone). *Carne trémula* attempts to dignify genre fiction (in this case crime novels) through national narrative (the history of Spain since the Dictatorship) and classical tragedy (spurned women and fatally competitive men). Finally, *Todo* elevates the sordid street scene (drugs and prostitution) to the aestheticized, abstracted realm of the theatrical stage.

But Almodóvar's resurrection of the art movie does not rely solely on this self-conscious incorporation of the debate on cultural value. It also appeals to aesthetic and commercial criteria which have repositioned the director within the Spanish cultural field. Thus, compared to the 'rose' films, the 'blue' films benefit from well-crafted screenplays, expert cinematography and music, and 'luxury' casts who bring with them echoes of past masters such as Buñuel. This increased formal perfection is in contrast with one anomalous trend of Spanish cinema of the 1990s whereby Almodóvar's films remained massively popular, but were no longer the very highest grossers in the domestic market. *Airbag, Torrente* and *Año Mariano* are typical of a late 1990s tendency towards wilfully grotesque farces which feature scatter-shot plotting, quick cutting to a rock soundtrack, and an appeal to new, eccentric or untested actors exemplified by Santiago Segura. By contrast with this very deliberate dumbness and apoliticism (which is, none the less, to be distinguished from the cheap farces of the past), Almodóvar's recent formal perfection and social commentary elevate his films, rendering them more culturally distinctive, and thus more available for critical consecration at home and abroad. Almodóvar's subjective dispositions (newly refined aesthetic choices in the films) thus coincide with objective positions (changes in the Spanish cultural field): the moribund art cinema, endangered at once culturally and commercially, is thus reborn in a perilous and provisional niche.

Just how perilous this niche is, is shown by the production and marketing history of *La flor*, which reveals the limits of Almodóvar's artistic autonomy in the mid-1990s. As a concept, *La flor*, the first of the 'blue period' films, was clearly well placed to take advantage of the changes in the Spanish audiovisual market I outlined earlier: the heroine Leo's shift up-market from pulp romance to serious fiction and, indeed, her contributions to the up-market daily *El País* that had previously panned Almodóvar's films coincide with the changing demographic appeal of Spanish cinema. Leo as character (middle-class, urban, educated and literate) herself embodies the female audience most likely to recognize themselves in Almodóvar's distinctive product. Likewise, the film's references to actuality (the war in the Balkans, the strikes and demonstrations at home), although newly prominent, are safely subordinate to the social and personal issues (work, home and love) that women readers claim in consumer surveys to prefer. Marisa Paredes also represents by virtue of her distinguished career in the theatre an added value of distinction that discriminating Spanish audiences would recognize.

While Almodóvar claimed when I interviewed him on the release of *La flor* that French co-producer Ciby played no part in the creative process, seeing the film only after its French version was completed (Smith 2000a: 177), other sources tell a slightly different story. It is true that producer-brother Agustín Almodóvar avoids domestic pre-selling of broadcasting rights, and that *Women on the Verge* 'allowed [Pedro] to break completely from a domestic market, and win an international following, albeit mostly on the arthouse circuit' (Finney 1996: 248). None the less, the 'green light' for Almodóvar's film was given by a French executive in Ciby's Paris office (249). International marketing also begins before the shoot. The sales agent in London reads a translation of the screenplay and makes estimates based on the current project, but dictated by previous business. Her view is unambiguous. The director is the 'key' selling point of his films abroad: 'When you're selling an Almodóvar movie, the star of the movie is Pedro, and that's what people want to buy.' Foreign markets are, however, variably resistant to the brand: Latin territories (France, Italy and South America) are strong, Germany is the toughest, while North America is unpredictable. Heavily marketed on sex, *High Heels* and *Kika* did poorly in the USA. Budgeted at $7 million, higher than Almodóvar's previous films of $5.5 million, *La flor* is thus a relatively tougher sell even to 'loyal Almodóvar distributors across the world'. While '50% of the world was pre-sold', North America and Germany were sold only on completion of the film (Sony Classics had seen an English version of the screenplay but preferred to wait). In these circumstances Ciby were still in the enviable position of covering their financial risk before the film opened.

The international sales officer has particular praise for one crucial form of marketing material that Almodóvar and El Deseo retain tight control over: still photography (250). Given the new visual austerity of *La flor* and the use of unspectacular interiors, set photography was less distinctive than before. But beyond the daily set photography, Almodóvar also stages special set-ups, and these are the ones which tend to make the marketing material: poster, press packs, trade photographs. The UK poster, featuring Paredes in a glamorous gown she did not wear in the film, resulted from just such a special set-up.

Another marketing matter personally supervised by Almodóvar is dubbing. The sales agent, however, believes that dubbing might alienate Almodóvar's loyal audience abroad: 'Whether you can break his films out to a wider audience by dubbing is debatable. Actually Almodóvar's work is pretty mainstream. It's an intelligent, sophisticated bill, but it's not inaccessible.' Box office performance was to prove the prediction correct: at 31 August 1996 *La flor* had grossed a respectable $14.6 million world-wide, of which, however, just $1 million was in the USA (251). What is significant about the production history of *La flor*, then, is not only that its 'Spanishness' is inseparable from its French funding and global pre-sales; it is that it blurs the divide, much clearer in other countries such as the UK, between art film and commercial cinema. Indeed, Almodóvar's own international sales agent calls his post-*Women* work both 'arthouse' and 'mainstream'. It would prove to be a difficult, but not impossible, balancing act for Almodóvar to follow in his next two films.

Almodóvar: three themes

A talent for outrageous orthodoxy.

(Boyero 1999)

Let us look at how the three themes that I mentioned earlier (homosexuality, literarity and urbanism) interact with this miraculous revival.

Sex

As we have seen, 'sexual topics' constituted one of the defining issues in *Variety*'s account of a declining genre, and in the 1980s gay content was vital to the marketing of Almodóvar's films to a niche foreign audience. Now that such themes have entered the US mainstream to some extent, they are less able to serve as a distinctive sign of cultural quality or audience selectivity. In Spain itself social changes have also rendered queer content more mainstream. Recent debates over gays in the military, civil union (with the *ley de parejas* failing by the narrowest of margins), the emergence of gay ghettos and bookshops in major cities, and the coming out of public figures such as Nacho Duato, director of the National Ballet, make the cultural climate very different from that of the 1980s. Moreover, an indigenous queer theory is beginning to make itself felt.

But, to adopt terms used by Leo Bersani (1995) in the very different US context, this gay presence, or spectacular visibility, is countered by a gay absence, or silence, in Almodóvar's blue period: the three films feature not one identifiable gay male character. *La flor* focuses on Angel (Juan Echanove), a sexless companion for Leo; *Carne* fetishizes the body of young delinquent Víctor (Liberto Rabal), but neglects the opportunities for same-sex eroticism in its prison and sport settings; and *Todo* boasts a powerful lesbian (Marisa Paredes's Huma Roja) and a versatile transsexual (Antonia San Juan's La Agrado). But if, as Stephen Maddison (2000) has argued, Manuela's teenage son Esteban is clearly coded as gay, with his love of Bette Davis, Truman Capote and Tennessee Williams, then he is eliminated early on by accidental death, serving merely as the initial sacrifice required for his mother's subsequent, hard-won rebirth.

Intellectual work on homosexuality in Spain is equally problematic. While Spain has finally produced an indigenous queer theory, it remains, like Spanish cinema, ambiguously indebted to foreign models. Two pioneering journals, which both began publishing in 2000, reveal the diversity and particularity of the intellectual labour that is parallel to Almodóvar's filmic practice. *Reverso* (billed as 'review of lesbian, gay, bisexual, transsexual, transgender . . . studies') characteristically takes as its theme 'the production of silence', while *Orientaciones* (subtitle: 'review of homosexualities') favours 'the law'.[5] The first is more literary in flavour, hosting a translated Judith Butler on 'the contagious word'; the latter more social, featuring Bourdieu on 'true juridical equality'. Looking more closely, however, a further distinction arises. While US queer theory was articulated around a largely phantom conflict between essence and construct (phantom because no scholar ever confessed belief in a homosexual identity that transcended time and space), Spaniards engaged in an equally bitter, but more puzzling, debate on equality and difference. Ironically, this proved to be the source of splits between gay activist groups, just as it was the rock on which Spanish feminism foundered some twenty years earlier.

The proponents of equality, hardly disinterested, provide the following schema. 'Difference' activists advocate a lesbian and gay community, a distinct culture opposed to heterosexual culture and laying claim to its own history (Sánchez and Pérez 2000: 152). They stress the visibility of homophobia, thus promoting 'victimist pessimism' and creating a self-inflicted low self-esteem which they attempt to remedy through gay pride and the commercial palliative of the pink peseta. These emotive tactics lead to destructive outing, the self-segregation of the ghetto, and confrontation with others. 'Equality' activists differ in both methods and results. Promoting citizenship, rather than community, they attempt to eliminate homophobia by invoking the common history of oppression and stressing social optimism. Against low self-esteem, they offer positive images and solidarity with other groups. This rational response includes 'respect for privacy' and leads, ideally, to *convivencia* or integration and tolerance and respect for all.

Now the association of the quest for 'community' with pessimism, segregation and confrontation is a curious one for an English-speaker. Indeed, the equality spokespeople take care to distinguish themselves from very visible Anglo-American models: writing 'gai' with an 'i', attacking massive Washington demonstrations which achieve no practical advance in US legislation, and proclaiming that the flamboyant new ghetto of Chueca must be opened up to all. It falls to their opposite numbers in *Reverso* to celebrate visibility in, say, Eduardo Mendicutti's moving short story on the coming out of Nacho Duato.

What I would suggest, however, is that, unlikely as this may seem, the newly austere Almodóvar coincides closely with the pragmatic and responsible egalitarians. For while Almodóvar refuses to refer to those undramatic and, indeed, uncinematic legal victories won or almost won by Spanish gradualist gays (military integration and civil union), he clearly shares their preference for citizenship over community. *La flor* celebrates new forms of solidarity, ending with Leo toasting her male friend Angel. *Carne* frankly hymns democracy, proclaiming at its close that Spaniards are 'no longer afraid' as they were under Franco. More transparently, *Todo* promotes *convivencia* quite literally: the mobile Manuela (a heterosexual woman) improvises new living arrangements with a transsexual, a pregnant nun and her family, and the HIV+ child fathered by her former partner, also a transsexual. Strangely silent on the specific topic of a male homosexuality that was newly visible in the Spanish society of the 1990s, Almodóvar is vocal and optimistic on the possibilities for tolerance and respect amongst the varied groups who share a common history of oppression. It is a modest and serious ambition appropriate to the muted and distinctive cinematic means of the blue period, and one that clearly chimes with Almodóvar's reconfigured, select audience both nationally and internationally.

This mainstreaming of the queer remains highly problematic. Writing in *El Mundo*, Carlos Boyero (1999) angrily rejects *Todo* as 'a universe exclusivly populated by lesbians, junkies, tranvestites . . . and other kinds of homosexuals . . . a complex, faithful, and collective portrait of daily life in which my heterosexuality . . . is ignored, scorned, or does not exist'. What Boyero attacks is the attempted universalization of the queer, which he takes to form part of Almodóvar's strategy in representing Spain as a whole. Similar attacks on Almodóvar's supposed exclusivism focused on his attention to women (Walker 1999). Yet the critical and commercial success of *Todo*, both at home and abroad, proved that queerness had indeed succeeded in serving just such a symbolic function, one that reconciled national narrative with marginal milieu through the prestige medium of cultural distinction. The theme of homosexuality thus at once invoked memories of sexual content once confined to the rarefied reaches of the arthouse and confirmed recent social changes evident, but not unchallenged, in contemporary society.

Literature

There is thus a particularly charged connection between homosexuality and literarity. The US writers invoked so solemnly in *Todo*, Truman Capote and Tennessee Williams, are of course famously gay writers; and their middle-brow status amongst English-speaking audiences is elevated in a Spain where they remain less familiar. Likewise, the primary model for *Todo*, *All About Eve*, is at once a camp classic and a highly literate work by Joseph L. Mankiewicz, a middle-brow director who is frequently attacked by English-speaking critics for favouring the verbal at the expense of the visual.

I have suggested that literarity functions as a privileged pointer to both Almodóvar's new cultural distinction and the relatively select domestic public for Spanish film. One scholar in the field of English literature, however, goes further in taking *Todo* seriously as a contribution to, or intervention in, literary studies and relating the film to the tastes of the English-speaking audiences of the arthouse. Stephen Maddison, who, we remember, cited the teenage Esteban as a crypto-gay character, contrasts Almodóvar's emphatic replaying of the final scene of *Streetcar* with previous prominent productions (2000: 266). At the close of Elia Kazan's film version of 1951, Blanche is plainly mad, her sister Stella has withdrawn upstairs, and her brutish husband Stanley is potentially able to 'seduce [her] back down again' (267). The CBS telefilm of 1995, starring Jessica Lange, is yet more conservative: Stella allows herself to be comforted by Stanley, and the brutal expulsion of Blanche facilitates the reconciliation of the heterosexual couple.

As Maddison notes, in Almodóvar's version Stella is by no means acquiescent, walking out on Stanley with their baby for good and leaving him to the homosocial pleasures of his drinking buddies (267). And, as in Williams's original, Almodóvar's Blanche is not mad but distressed. Not only, then, is heterosexuality intolerable for Almodóvar's women, as, arguably, it is for Williams's; they also have choices outside of relations with men: Nina, the actress playing Stella is, of course, in love with Huma's Blanche. Later, Manuela, who also fled an abusive husband with a baby, will take on the role of Stella, for one night only. Almodóvar's reinterpretation, an act of explicit literary criticism, thus reaffirms in its new plot points the 'emotional and cultural affiliation between women and gay men' which Maddison also sees in Almodóvar's continuing and much publicized intimacies with his leading ladies (270). Maddison sees this 'heterosocial' coupledom not as closetry, but rather (like the Spanish egalitarians who praise and prize solidarity) as a 'resituation of ... female identification in the context of gay dissidence' (272).

Proof of the anxiety caused by even such understated strategies is Anglo-American critics' struggle to reconcile female affiliation with the cultural capital commensurate with Almodóvar's literary references. Indeed, the two prove mutually contradictory: if 'Almodóvar is now a great filmmaker [it is] because he has moved on from the camp, melodramatic female identification for which he became famous' (271). In the words of the conservative UK broadsheet the *Telegraph*, 'ditching excess ... and kitschy hysteria in favour of moderate, fine-grained story telling' (271), Almodóvar gains access to an arthouse clearly defined in literary or narrative terms only at the cost of leaving his coded queerness at the entrance.

Paradoxically, such queerness is, for foreign audiences at least, as much a criterion of selectivity as is literary allusion. On the one hand, 'in the UK and America Almodóvar's audiences of gays and lesbians, along with middle-class, professionalized, university educated, broadsheet-reading constituencies do not understand the writer and director's sexuality as problematic . . . Rather, we might imagine his queerness . . . to be positively part of his appeal to an audience anxious to secure its class authority through its cosmopolitan sophistication' (270). On the other hand, Maddison continues, repeating *Variety*'s conflation of art movies and foreign films, 'the appreciation of art-house cinema [by Almodóvar's Anglo-American audiences] signifies their liberalism and thus enables them to acquire the kind of metropolitan cultural capital that distinguishes them from their suburban equivalents' (269). Literarity thus plays a key role in reconciling the competing criteria of queerness and greatness, whose combination continues to cause metropolitan critics, if not audiences, such anxiety.

Carne trémula also relies on literary antecedents which aim to confer cultural distinction on the popular: both Ruth Rendell, whose novel is the only one that Almodóvar has claimed to adapt, and co-screenwriter Ray Loriga, whose spare, economical style replays US hard-boiled genre fiction with conspicuous success. Like Rendell and Loriga, then, Almodóvar wagers on distinction, separating himself from the popular herd even as he incorporates its formal and material strategies. This 'bet' was riskier in the case of *Carne* than in other films, as a production history in trade journal *Screen International* reveals (Puente 1997). At $4.4 million, *Carne* was 'one of Almodóvar's most expensive films', co-produced by Agustín Almodóvar with Ciby 2000. While Agustín had by this time given up on the US market ('we practically don't think of [it]'), success with the 'usual audience' (given as Spain, Italy and France, then Latin America and the Far East) was compromised by Pedro's abandonment of his 'regular stable of actors' for such young stars as Javier Bardem and neophyte Liberto Rabal (established box office attraction Jorge Sainz had been dropped two days into the ten-week shoot). Marketing thus focused on moulding the image of the new male star (one press shot even showed Pedro holding Rabal's face in his hand) and attracting literary kudos: heavyweight Cuban exile novelist Guillermo Cabrera Infante wrote a lengthy piece in *El País* (1997) praising the film's 'diversity of drama' and 'technical perfection'. In its review, *Screen International* told its insider readers that *Carne* 'offers dedicated arthousers many of those hedonistic pleasures that first made foreign films such a guilty treat' (Brown 1997). Pleasure and profit are thus held in unstable combination.

Here I would like to back up my argument for Almodóvar's literary resurrection of the arthouse with reference to an unlikely authority: André Bazin, the austere moralist of cinematic realism and still a touchstone for the definition of film art or art film. Although his theory is, as is well known, based on the ontology of the filmic image (the trace of the real on celluloid), Bazin is equally sensitive to the literary. Indeed, he claims that 'the aesthetic of the Italian [neo-realist] cinema . . . is simply the equivalent on film of the American novel' (Bazin 1967: 39). Just as Welles and Rossellini, stylistically so different, are structurally similar in their relation to the 'image fact' (38), so Italian cinema combines the 'demon of melodrama' (31) with 'reportage' in a way that problematizes 'rank[ing] the genre . . . in the aesthetic hierarchy' (33). Although Bazin has no doubt that such films as *Paisà* exhibit 'an aesthetic of narrative that is both complex and original' (34), he does not deny that they include literary or melodramatic elements apparently at odds with his aesthetics of ontology.

The case of Almodóvar is strikingly similar, poised as he is between the visual and the verbal, the cinematic and the theatrical. It is this magical and paradoxical conflation which can cause such highly stylized films to possess what Bazin calls 'this perfect and natural adherence to actuality' (20).

City

It is here that the question of the city is of the essence. I noted earlier that the shift from the rose period to the blue is also that between positive and negative representations of urban life. But the increasing stylization of Almodóvar's films is not incompatible with a social commentary which, if not Rossellini-style reportage, does engage with lived reality. Once more Bazin, the famous champion of location shooting (or 'raw, natural settings' (28)), is unexpectedly helpful here:

> The Italian city, ancient or modern, is prodigiously photogenic. From antiquity, Italian city planning has remained theatrical and decorative. City life is a spectacle, a commedia dell'arte that the Italians stage for their own pleasure. And even in the poorest quarters of the town, the corral-like groupings of the houses, thanks to the terraces and balconies, offer outstanding possibilities for spectacle. (28–9)

I would argue that Spanish urbanism, like Italian, is always already spectacle, enabling Almodóvar to combine the aesthetic abstraction of the theatre with the social concreteness of reportage most strikingly in the rapturous yet respectful vision of Barcelona displayed in *Todo*.

Moreover, what is notable about the blue period films is that for the first time Almodóvar exploits the spectacular monuments of Spain's rival metropolises, Madrid and Barcelona. *La flor* climaxes in an eerily empty, but seductively lit, Plaza Mayor, in which Leo and Angel achieve emotional intimacy; *Carne*'s opening credits play over the Puerta de Alcalá, the triumphal arch built to celebrate the entrance of Carlos III into Madrid; *Todo* lingers on the Sagrada Familia, spectacular icon of Barcelona's religious and national aspirations. All three loaded locations are inseparable from Spain's political and civic history, whether Hapsburg absolutism, Bourbon Enlightenment or Catalan revivalism. But such familiar icons carry with them the illusory transparency of what Henri Lefebvre calls 'abstract space'. Glimpsed as they are in the films at night and at speed from motorcycle or taxi, they at once demonstrate and negate state power, evacuating time from the city and provoking history only as 'nostalgia' (Lefebvre 1991: 51).

The heritage of statist violence in such monuments as Felipe III's Plaza Mayor, whose current tourists and stamp collectors belie its earlier use as a spectacular setting for *autos-da-fé*, is thus erased. As Lefebvre puts it in *The Right to the City*, population centres are mocked by their most visible structures, monuments which remain uninhabited and indeed uninhabitable (1996: 112). Just as Almodóvar cites literary classics, appropriating their prestige, so he incorporates urban monuments into the fabric of his blue period features, colluding with their very visible authority.

Moreover, during the period in which these films were made, Madrid and Barcelona were successfully marketed around Europe as weekend tourist destinations, eclipsing more traditional favourites such as Vienna and Venice. Erasing memories of cut-price Costa beach holidays, Spain repositioned itself as a centre of up-market cultural tourism. The recent prominence of such newly recognizable images shows once more how Almodóvar managed to intersect with the changing consumer habits of his metropolitan audience. Cultural capital merges with capitals of culture: in tourism and art movie alike, urban distinction is successfully sold to foreign aesthetes.

These newly visible monuments are, however, juxtaposed with less recognizable, more heterogeneous spaces: the schoolyard glimpsed from Leo's apartment in *La flor* (an authentic and unexceptional location); *Carne*'s ruinous shanties in the shadow of the gate-like Kío Towers (an ironic echo of the equally grand and empty Puerta de Alcalá); the crowded multiracial corners of *Todo*'s working-class Raval. The street is thus, in Lefebvre's terms once more, an appropriated space, with its own rhythms and uses (1991: 131): in *La flor* it pulses suddenly and inexplicably with the demonstrations of striking public health workers; in *Carne* it is the setting for both the grimy and furtive low lifes glimpsed from the police car at the start and the colourful shoppers framed in a final festive crane shot. Even the waste ground by Nou Camp in *Todo* (re-created outside Madrid), an infernal edge city in which cruising cars slowly circle showy transsexual prostitutes, embodies a spontaneous rearticulation of space, a new practice improvised at the limits of urbanism and unconstrained by past history. It is a fragile and provisional 'queer site'.

Overwhelmingly, however, Almodóvar confirms Lefebvre's intuition, hostile to postmodern praise of the periphery, that the right to the city is inseparable from centrality: 'there is no urban reality without a centre' (1996: 195). And the blue period clearly shows how the most monumental of Spanish city centres can continue to be reappropriated by their inventive citizens. Both *La flor* and *Carne* celebrate the Gran Vía, originally Madrid's most ambitious attempt to imitate Haussmanian abstract geometry and now saturated with faded civic ambitions from Alfonso XIII to Franco. The grand corner of the Plaza del Callao, half-way down the Gran Vía's length, is glimpsed only behind Leo's bed as she recovers in Angel's apartment high above street level, the great avenue diminished and domesticated. At the grand intersection of the Gran Vía with the calle de Alcalá, the bronze figure of the Winged Victory above the Metrópolis building is reread by Víctor's teenage mother (Penélope Cruz). As she is giving birth on a bus in the empty, spectral Madrid of a Francoist curfew, she believes it is an 'angel' about to fall to earth. Once more, the monument is humanized, the human sacralized. In *Todo*, the Sagrada Familia, shown explicitly through Manuela's eyes, dignifies maternal loss, while the new Hospital del Mar is visited by the pregnant Sister Rosa (also played by Cruz). With its glass walls open on to the intensively used beach, the hospital integrates solidarity and festivity, reviving a degraded urban landscape. Such reappropriations of space, shared by Almodóvar and some of the more successful town planners, protect and promote the distinctive quality of an urbanism that is as fragile and valuable as 'niche' art cinema.

Journalists made much of Almodóvar's tardy transfer from Madrid to Barcelona, evidence surely of his untiring quest for distinctive and spectacular visual pleasures. And in spite of *Todo*'s transparent indifference to the particularity of Catalan culture, the local press seemed flattered by Almodóvar's attention, documenting the varied locations of the shoot and proclaiming that his single film had done more for Catalan film than the entire production of the locally based industry (Casarín 1999; Bonet Mojica 1999). What went unnoticed, yet is more striking, perhaps, is that the Barcelona visited by Almodóvar, however dense and glamorous, was no longer at the cutting edge of urbanism. Consecrated by the annual award of the Royal Institute of British Architects in 2000 (given uniquely to the city as a whole), Barcelona was dismissed the following year by trend-setting trade magazine *Blueprint*, which argued that no innovative architecture had been commissioned since the *annus mirabilis* of 1992 (Hattersley 2001).[6] Significantly, the same issue of *Blueprint* carried a eulogy of Madrid–London-based graphic designer Fernando Gutiérrez (originator of *El País* listings supplement *Las Tentaciones*, now promoted to Benetton's *Colors* (Buxton 2001)) and avant-garde architect Rem Koolhaas's praise of Lagos, a West African city whose lack of the rational infrastructure so successfully instituted by Barcelona makes it a model of tense, congested and extreme urbanism (Koolhaas 2001), far indeed from the cool rationalism of the Hospital del Mar. We have seen that, newly austere and moderate and in synch with reconfigured Spanish cinema audiences, Almodóvar coincides with the modest ambitions of gay equality activists and middle-brow *littérateurs* (Mankiewicz and Williams). Echoing his strategies with regard to sex and literature, Almodóvar also pitches his vision of the city to a distinctive clientele: educated enough to recognize the reappropriation of old monuments and the clean, classical lines of newish developments, but unfamiliar with, or unsympathetic to, the latest and most challenging trends in design and urbanism.

Exceptional culture

Mother of the Year.

(Gopalan 1999)

On the US release of *Todo*, a brief article in monthly *Premiere* (under the rubric 'Indie Exposure') rehearsed with unusual concision the contradictory characteristics of the arthouse in the 1990s (Gopalan 1999). Abandoning the 'sexual content' that had made him an 'enfant terrible', Almodóvar now, we are told, focuses on 'masterful storytelling . . . festooned with resonant references'. The author even sees a 'Shakespearean dimension' in the film: 'men dressed as women, bawdy jokes, and melodrama'. But while the journalist writes that *Todo* is typical of Almodóvar's 'trio of recent dramas' ('thoughtful, melancholy'), Almodóvar claims, ironically perhaps, that 'the audience matured – I remained the same'. Hence the colourful 1980s 'back-drop' is intact, but the 'shock value' has diminished. The reciprocal relation between *auteur* and audience and the changing status of sexual topics could hardly be clearer.

In Spain media coverage over *Todo*'s nomination for the foreign-language Oscar demonstrated, as ever, that Spanish film was an endangered species even in its home country, longing for recognition by a Hollywood which most critics affected none the less to despise. Moreover, the illness and subsequent death of Almodóvar's own mother prompted an ambiguous campaign of solidarity from the industry: Almodóvar's distributors placed press ads saying they were 'with [Pedro]; now more than ever'. This was, in Maddison's terms, a 'heterosocial' move: like the ambivalent press focus on the closeness of Almodóvar's relationships with his leading ladies, the stress on his love for his mother served safely to distract attention from his private life, which remained inviolate.

Reports on the location shooting of *Todo* (invariably run under the title 'Almodóvar's Barcelona') gave rise to detailed Catalan press coverage offering minute anecdotes of city life: the intruder in the Plaça Medinaceli obsessed with becoming a 'chico Almodóvar' who eventually had to be thrown off the shoot; the elderly ladies off the Carrer Princesa who continued to sit on the same bench as Almodóvar prepared his lengthy and perfectionist street scenes (Casarín 1999). Such references to actuality cut against US press coverage, which (as in *Premiere*) stressed the literary and aesthetic values of the deracinated arthouse: *Variety* noted that the film was 'studded with references to 50's melodrama', and claimed that the 'detailed lensing' was 'high risk arty', distracting from the realism of the urban settings (Holland 1999).

This was characteristic of a growing split in reception between Europe and the USA, at both commercial and cultural levels. For example, *Carne* had grossed $1.5 million in Italy after three weeks, and $2 million in France after four weeks. In the USA *La flor* took fourteen weeks to take just $800,000. In his study of the policy of 'cultural exception', Frédéric Depétris notes a recent 'dualization' of goals in the French audiovisual sector, now 'split between its will to create a self-sustaining European audiovisual industry, able to compete globally and win a far greater share of the European market and its cultural goal of producing "art films" and to create a more "cineliterate" population, through education, in its widest sense, in order to secure an audience for such films' (Depétris 2000). While Almodóvar may be the European filmmaker closest to realizing these twin ambitions, his place in the Spanish film industry, much weaker in its own territory than the French, paradoxically puts him in a stronger position to realize the double French goals: making cine-literate films for a smaller, more select home audience, films that also have some commercial success abroad.

Hence, in the ambiguous and endangered figure of the arthouse, Almodóvar repositions himself within both the Spanish cultural field and the international audiovisual marketplace. The aesthetic tendency towards the pursuit of cultural capital combines with the social tendency towards the analysis of sex, literature and the city, areas which have themselves been transformed over the course of Almodóvar's career. Walking the aesthetic and industrial tightrope between niche market and mainstream, austerity and excess, Almod-óvar thus reanimates past *auteurs* in the new, less forgiving environment of the millennium, in which both subjective attitudes towards the art movie and objective conditions towards its distribution and exhibition are increasingly unfavourable. Still the ghosts of Fellini, Truffaut and Kurosawa are resurrected in Almodóvar's blue period, a uniquely poised attempt to combine artistic and economic ambitions.

Notes

1 The scarcity of directors thus contrasts with the excessive number of features released, which *Variety* calls 'overkill'.
2 Ciment's view was contested by two other participants, British director Mike Figgis and critic Jonathan Romney.
3 See my analysis of SGAE data below.
4 Appropriately enough, *Les Inrockuptibles* has charted the same shift itself, from rebellious indie pop mag to sober but chic arts review.
5 My thanks to the editors of both journals: Jaime del Val and F. Javier Ugarte, respectively.
6 The magazine did acknowledge, however, that innovative projects had just been commissioned in the city to be completed by 2004.

References

Bazin, André (1967) *What is Cinema?*, vol. 2. Berkeley and Los Angeles: University of California Press.
Bersani, Leo (1995) *Homos*. Cambridge, MA: Harvard University Press.

Bonet Mojica, Lluís (1999) Evas al desnudo [review of *Todo sobre mi madre*]. *La Vanguardia*, 18 April.

Bourdieu, Pierre (1996) *The Rules of Art*. Cambridge: Polity.

—— (1999) Questions aux vrais maîtres du monde. *Le Monde*, 14 October.

Boyero, Carlos (1999) ¡Cuánto talento para la ortodoxia abusiva! [review of *Todo sobre mi madre*]. *El Mundo*, 16 April.

Brown, Colin (1997) Live Flesh (Carne trémula) [review]. *Screen International*, 17 October, p. 37.

Buxton, Pamela (2001) Double Spread [profile of graphic designer Fernando Gutiérrez]. *Blueprint*, January, pp. 46–9.

Cabrera Infante, Guillermo (1997) La carne no es triste [review of *Carne trémula*]. *El País: Babelia*, 11 October, pp. 2–3.

Casarín, Albert (1999) La Barcelona d'Almodóvar. *Avui*, 16 April, pp. 4–6.

Cox, Dan, and Bing, Jonathan (2000) Art Movies: Overkill or Over-the-Hill? *Variety*, 2–8 October, pp. 1, 62–3.

Depétris, Frédéric (2000) Is 'Cultural Exception' an Answer to Globalization? Paper read at Conference on Globalization and Cultural Diversity in Europe, Notre Dame University 8–9 December (unpaginated).

Finney, Angus (1996) *The State of European Cinema: A New Dose of Reality*. London: Cassell.

Gopalan, Nisha (1999) 'Mother' of the Year [interview with Almodóvar]. *Premiere*, December, p. 81.

Green, Jennifer (2001) Spanish Production Booms despite Flat B[ox] O[ffice]. *Screen International*, 19 January, p. 10.

Hattersley, Lia (2001) Raw Talent [Barcelona architecture round-up]. *Blueprint*, January, pp. 30–4.

Holland, Jonathan (1999) All about My Mother [review]. *Variety*, 19–25 April, p. 47.

ICA (1999) Art Cinema: Where Next? programme for day conference, 9 October (unpaginated).

Koolhaas, Rem (2001) City Limits. *Blueprint*, January, pp. 42–4.

Lefebvre, Henri (1991) *The Production of Space*. Oxford: Blackwell.

—— (1996) *The Right to the City*. Oxford: Blackwell.

Maddison, Stephen (2000) All About Women: Pedro Almodóvar and the Heterosocial Dynamic. *Textual Practice*, 14 (2), pp. 265–84.

Orientaciones: revista de homosexualidades (2000), no. 1.

Ostria, Vincent (1999) Peace & Love [interview with Almodóvar]. *Les Inrockuptibles*, 19–25 May, pp. 32–5.

Puente, David (1997) Live Flesh [production report], *Screen International*, 28 February, p. 27.

Reverso: revista de estudios lesbianos, gays, bisexuales, transexuales, transgénero . . . (2000), no. 1.

Sánchez, Miguel Angel and Pérez, Pedro A. (2000) Los caminos del Movimiento Lésbico y Gai. *Orientaciones*, 1, pp. 149–57.

Smith, Paul Julian (1994) *Desire Unlimited: The Cinema of Pedro Almodóvar*. London: Verso.

—— (2000a) *Desire Unlimited: The Cinema of Pedro Almodóvar*, revised, expanded edition. London: Verso.

—— (2000b) *The Moderns: Time, Space, and Subjectivity in Contemporary Spanish Culture*. Oxford: Oxford University Press.

Sociedad General de Autores y Editores (2000) *Hábitos de consumo cultural*. Madrid: SGAE.

Walker, Alexander (1999) Into the Sex Change Room [review of *Todo sobre mi madre*]. *Evening Standard* [London], 26 August, p. 29.

Index

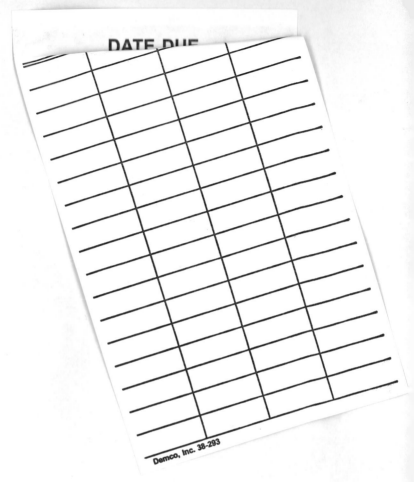

DATE DUE

Demco, Inc. 38-293